The Anxiety Cure:
37 Science-Based (5-Minute) Methods to Beat Back the Blues, Stay Positive, and Finally Relax

by Nick Trenton
www.NickTrenton.com

Table of Contents

CHAPTER 1: DAILY HABITS FOR HAPPINESS — 7

HAVE A ROUTINE—BUT NOT A STRICT ONE!	9
SAY THANK YOU	13
MEDITATION CAN MAKE YOU HAPPY	16
SELF-TALKING YOURSELF TO HAPPINESS	21
THE READING HABIT	27
DEAR HAPPINESS ...	31
KEEP THE FLAME OF HOPE BURNING	34

CHAPTER 2: QUICK HAPPINESS FIXES — 39

WHAT MAKES A HAPPY SONG HAPPY?	40
INJECTING HAPPINESS	46
EAT ICE CREAM	52
RELIVE HAPPY MEMORIES	55
EFT TAPPING	63
FLOWER POWER	68

CHAPTER 3: PROVEN HAPPINESS METHODS AND TECHNIQUES — 74

THE HAPPINESS BEHIND POSITIVE ANTICIPATION	74
TAKE A PHOTO WITH YOUR SMARTPHONE	79
UNPLUG: YOUR BRAIN NEEDS A BREAK FROM SCREENS	82
APPRECIATE ART ... OR MAKE SOME YOURSELF	86
DECLUTTER	90
GETTING RID OF DIGITAL CLUTTER: NOTIFICATIONS	93

CHAPTER 4: CREATING A HAPPY ENVIRONMENT 101

Green: The Shade of Happiness 102
You Feel Good When You Get Enough Zzz's 106
Dogs, Cats, and Happiness 109
A Quick Workout Can Turn Your Mood Around 115
Be Happy in Style 120
The Magic of Scented Candles 124
Adjust Your Lighting 126

CHAPTER 5: THE SOCIAL SIDE OF HAPPINESS 131

Happiness Is a Call Away 131
Sing with Others 138
Mix up Some Happiness in a Bowl 143
The PERMA Model 147
Drop Black-and-White Thinking 155
Master the Art of Complaining 159
Stop Counterfactual Thinking 163

CHAPTER 6: YOUR BRAIN AND HAPPINESS 169

People Get Happier as They Age 169
Play Video Games 173
Watch a Sad Movie 178
Buy Something New 183
Prioritize Future Happiness, Prioritize Positivity 192
DOSE Hormones 197

SUMMARY GUIDE 205

Chapter 1: Daily Habits for Happiness

In the whirlwind of our modern lives, anxiety and overthinking have become constant companions. The incessant chatter of our minds, filled with worries, doubts, and endless hypotheticals, can leave us feeling overwhelmed, restless, and discontented. It seems that no matter how hard we try, the pursuit of peace and contentment eludes us.

But what if there was a way to break free from the grip of anxiety and overthinking? What if we could silence the cacophony of our minds and discover a path toward tranquility, happiness, and fulfillment? This book explores precisely that journey—the transformative voyage from a life dominated by anxiety to one of profound calmness and contentment.

Through a blend of practical strategies, introspective exercises, and empowering perspectives, we pave the way toward embracing serenity and cultivating lasting happiness. The pages between this cover aim to guide you toward a newfound sense of peace. By providing practical tips and insight on how to manage anxiety and overthinking, you will uncover a path toward a more fulfilling and joyful life. We will also be looking at what happiness is, how it works physiologically, and how we can use current scientific understanding of well-being to start creating a life that we love. Happiness starts in the brain, but that doesn't mean it's just a question of neuroscience. We'll be exploring the question of happiness over the course of forty practical, evidence-based techniques, covering daily happiness habits, joy-inducing environments, and short-term quick fixes for bad days.

Finally, we'll consider how we can pull everything together to create lasting lifestyle changes that genuinely make us feel good. Let's dive in and discover the power of tackling our inner struggles and finding the happiness we all deserve.

Have a Routine—But Not a Strict One!

Having a routine is like having a roadmap to your day. It helps you prioritize tasks and plan out your time. But did you know that having a routine can also help ease anxiety? When everything feels uncertain and up in the air, having a sense of structure can be incredibly reassuring. It's like a warm hug from your schedule, telling you that everything will be okay.

Picture the kind of person you imagine has their life together. They wake up at the same time every day, they have an orderly morning routine, and they have a fixed food, work, and exercise schedule that they move through predictably, every day. They're probably quite productive . . . but are they happy?

It turns out that although routine can be beneficial, you don't want to get stuck in a rut. Research psychologist Catherine Hartley and her colleagues conducted a study with 132 participants who were tracked for three or four months. Hartley wanted to see their general mental health state and overall mood, as well as examine what kind of daily routines they engaged in.

What the data revealed was pretty interesting: People who were able to do something novel every day tended to report more positive, happy emotions than those who just stuck to the same old, same old. The novelty didn't have to be big—it could be something as simple as going to a new place or trying something different for lunch.

The team also tracked the participants via GPS and noticed that on days when people moved around more and visited more locations, they were more likely to use words like "happy," "relaxed," and "excited" to describe their mood that day.

Hartley wanted to understand more, so she had some of the participants undergo an MRI scan. Here, she found that the people who were regularly exposing themselves to novel situations actually had different brain function than those who didn't. Their scans showed an increase in brain activity between the hippocampus and the striatum—areas of the brain associated with experience processing and reward, respectively. The more diverse the experiences, the greater the connectivity between these two brain regions and the greater the reported feelings of well-being.

The team published their findings in the journal *Nature Neuroscience*, concluding that there was a definite relationship between our daily environments, our behaviors, our brain activity, and our overall mood. Diversity of experience, they found, was positively correlated with improved well-being.

"Our results suggest that people feel happier when they have more variety in their daily routines—when they go to novel places and have a wider array of experiences," Hartley claimed, and since the research concluded just before worldwide Covid-19 lockdowns, many were interested in using the findings to maintain well-being despite being shut in at home.

If "experiential diversity" means greater well-being, then it's obvious that if we want to be happier, we need a little novelty. What does that look like day to day?

Well, it's likely that each of us has different thresholds for what counts as "novel"—for some, new experiences can feel stressful or threatening, while others are major thrill-seekers and adrenaline junkies. What Hartley's research suggests, however, is that just a *little* daily variation is enough to wake up certain areas of the brain. You don't have to go on a grand adventure every day—just try something new here and there:

- Take a different route to work or, if you have a few minutes, explore that strange back street that you always walk past but never go down.
- Instead of getting your favorite dish at the restaurant you always go to, get something completely different or try another place entirely.
- Mix up the order of things you were already going to do that day; for example, change plans at the last minute and run some errands in town instead for a change of pace.
- Take a walk somewhere you haven't been before and really absorb everything new and unexpected around you.
- Rummage in your closet and wear something you've forgotten about or a novel combination of items you haven't tried before.
- Work in a different room, in a different chair, or even in the same room but oriented differently.

The reason novelty makes us happy is that, neurophysiologically, the sensation of novelty is closely connected to the sensation of reward. And in many ways, the experience of depression is not dissimilar from the feeling of being "stuck in a rut" and under-stimulated.

Trying something new is a way to kick yourself out of that rut.

Think of novelty as giving your brain a little surprise, which produces a tiny dopamine kick and engages you with your environment. If you're feeling a little low, pause and ask if you're really just bored—have you been doing too much of that same thing? Time to try something new!

Say Thank You

Gratitude is like a little magic potion that can help ease the gnawing knot of anxiety in your stomach. There's something about focusing on the things you're thankful for that just automatically boosts your mood and improves your outlook on everything. When you take a moment to feel genuinely grateful for something—whether it's a sense of safety, having a roof over your head, or even just the perfect cup of coffee in the morning—it helps shift your focus away from all the things that worry you. And when you're not constantly consumed by fear and anxiety, you're freer to feel calm, relaxed, and happy.

It's like a two-for-one special—you get to feel good about the things you have and also enjoy a little mental vacation from all the stressful thoughts swirling around in your head.

When you're feeling down, your attention is deliberately focused on everything that's wrong in your world. You amplify everything that's lacking while ignoring everything that is actually going well for you. One way to reverse this tendency is to use the power of gratitude.

Gratitude and thankfulness are having a moment right now, and for good reason—there is mounting evidence that simply being happy with what you've got is the key to being happy, period. This idea is not new, however, and it comes with predictable and measurable changes in the brain.

Dr. Prathik Kini had always been interested in the phenomenon of gratitude but specifically wanted to see what it looked like in the brain. In a 2015 experiment, he asked forty-three people who were already receiving psychotherapy for anxiety and depression to be his study participants. He broke them into two groups—one group was asked to write out "gratitude letters," while the other group simply continued with their therapy.

After three months, Kini put all the subjects through an MRI scan while they did a separate gratitude task called the "Pay It Forward" task. The subjects were told that a generous sponsor had given them some money, before being asked if they wanted to donate a portion of this money in turn as a way of saying thank you. It was explained that they should donate money in proportion to how grateful they felt for the money they had received. So, if they felt extremely grateful for the gift, they were told to donate generously. The researchers did this so they could assign exact numbers to the measurement of gratitude, which is understandably a little hard to quantify.

The results were interesting. Kini discovered that there were significant differences in brain activity in the participants who agreed to donate some of their money versus those who decided not to do so. But there was more: "Subjects who participated in gratitude letter writing showed both behavioral increases in gratitude and significantly greater neural modulation in the medial prefrontal cortex three months later." Basically, they found that, when people had previously strengthened feelings of gratitude by writing gratitude letters, they tended to experience the effects of the Pay It Forward exercise weeks and even months after.

We can conclude two things from this research:

1. Gratitude literally shapes our brain, and

2. the more we practice gratitude, the more grateful we become.

And though it wasn't the focus of this research, we can also see that the more grateful we feel, the more generous we tend to want to be. This makes sense—if you feel blessed and like you have more than you need, you are more likely to feel that you're in the position to share. Though many other studies have shown that gratitude can make you healthier, more resilient, and happier, and it can even help you have better willpower, Kini et al. showed that gratitude actually leads to concrete, physical changes in the brain.

Injecting a little gratitude, like novelty, doesn't have to be a major project to be effective. Occasionally write a letter to someone who has done something to benefit your life, or keep a gratitude journal noting everything you're fortunate to have. Why not wake up every morning and simply say "thank you" that you're alive today?

Meditation Can Make You Happy

Have you ever had one of those days where everything just seems to go wrong? The kind of day where you spill coffee on your shirt, get stuck in traffic, and forget an important meeting? Let's face it, life can be stressful.

That's why more and more people are turning to meditation to find a sense of calm and happiness. Research has shown that regular meditation can decrease anxiety and increase feelings of well-being (Thorpe, 2023). By taking a few minutes each day to quiet your mind and focus on your breath, you can reduce stress levels and improve your mood.

Many of us already know that meditating is the gold standard when it comes to self-regulation, discipline, lowering anxiety, and stress relief, to name a few benefits. But one of the most underappreciated effects of a regular meditation practice is simple: You just feel good. Researchers led by Richard Davidson at the University of Wisconsin-Madison have taken a closer look at how meditation can specifically affect our sense of compassion and empathy for others. Increased compassion, they reasoned, directly enhances our own well-being and happiness.

Davidson and his research team wanted to investigate whether meditators are happier in life. Compassion for all beings sounds nice, but does it have any physiological correlations in the brain? The team gathered Buddhist monks who were meditation veterans, as well as non-meditators, and looked at their brain function using fMRIs. These scans allow scientists to see the brain's function in real time, as well as follow the person's reaction to various stimuli as it unfolds in the brain. The researchers subjected the participants to all kinds of stimuli, including extremely distracting and distressing ones, like the sounds of screams and jackhammers.

They did indeed find that the Buddhists had consistently greater activity in the brain's "happiness centers" and that they were less disturbed by upsetting stimuli. The Buddhists had greater activity in the part of the brain called the insula, which is what allows the mind to have an internal "map" of the various organs of the body, and the anterior cingulate cortices, which allow us to feel empathy for another's pain (Lutz et al., 2008).

It appeared that meditators had greatly moderated responses to stimuli compared to the control subjects. This has some intriguing implications for practitioners who claim that meditation allows them literally to influence and change their bodies.

The Enigula and the temporoparietal junction are other areas in the brain that showed greater activity in the meditators—these regions are associated with emotions, empathy, and the ability to perspective shift. It appeared that brain activity associated with joy and serenity were more pronounced in those who meditated.

The researchers even discovered elevated levels of gene-regulating machinery and lower expression of pro-inflammatory genes after eight hours of meditation. Practically speaking, this implies faster recovery and better stress resilience.

The researchers concluded that the practice of meditation enabled "epigenetic alterations of the genome." Jill Sakai claimed in the journal *Psychoneuroendocrinology* that "gene expression changes with meditation." In other words, though meditation cannot change your genes, it can influence the way those genes are expressed.

Importantly, the kind of meditation under study was one focused on compassion and emerged from the Buddhist conception of loving kindness for all beings. But it is also possible to meditate with "pure compassion" that is not directed to anyone in particular, and this has also been associated with greater well-being and improved health.

Researchers at the University of California San Francisco Medical Center found that the areas of the brain associated with happiness were more active in meditators, and the areas associated with fear—i.e., parts of the amygdala—appeared to be better modulated. So, overall, the evidence strongly suggests that meditating Buddhists really are happier than others, not to mention less disturbed by negative stimuli.

How can we meditate to improve our happiness? Meditation master Dzongsar Khyentse Rinpoche warns against the kind of trendy Western meditation that is really mindfulness "with a focus," i.e., pushing some experiences and thoughts out of awareness in order to focus on one chosen thought or object. Instead of this busy, grasping form of meditation, he suggests not doing anything in particular with your body, breath, or mind. Don't "focus" on anything. Sit erect but relaxed, cross-legged but without strain. Keep your eyes open and your gaze soft and possibly lowered, not forcing it on anything.

Next, your breathing: Each time your breath goes out, "go out with it." Whatever you're feeling in that moment as your breath leaves you, let your mind dissolve with it. Don't count breaths or follow the inhale or force yourself to do any kind of special "spiritual" breathing. Just be natural and let go of any struggle. See if you can identify completely with this breath rather than imagining it is separate from you. After the breath out dissolves, there is a gap, and you are surrounded by space. Just hang there and linger for a moment. The inhale will happen by itself.

When you've done this for a while, try to pair the body and the breath. Practitioners are advised to have a "strong back; soft front." Good posture represents your innate dignity and strength, and dissolving with the breath represents vulnerability, softness, and compassion.

Your mind will get in the way, but remember that you are not trying to stop thought—it's a battle you'll always lose! Thoughts are not the problem but rather our attachment to them. Instead of getting fixated on our own thought traffic, we can just be aware and see thoughts as thoughts. We just notice when our minds have wandered, but without irritation (which is just one more thought).

Simply sit. Body, breath, and mind. Be this way for a few minutes, then get up to stretch your legs.

Self-Talking Yourself to Happiness

Meditation is something we can practice and deepen over the course of years—or a whole lifetime—and it's also something we can dip into literally any moment of any day. So much of our unhappiness manifests and expresses itself as thoughts. Our constant flow of mental chatter can be, when we start to look at it, surprisingly negative and repetitive. During meditation, you may be surprised to find just how relentless your inner self-talk really is.

But could you change the program, so to speak?

Most of us have heard of the technique of self-affirmation. Have you ever stopped to give yourself a compliment? It may sound silly, but taking the time to acknowledge your strengths and accomplishments can actually work wonders for your overall well-being. Self-affirmation is a simple practice that involves focusing on your positive qualities and achievements. It is when you use self-talk to affirm your own worth, to support yourself, to show yourself kindness, and to boost your appreciation of your own value as a human being. Basically, it's speaking nicely to yourself!

By reminding ourselves of our worth, we can lower feelings of anxiety about the future and foster a sense of calm and happiness. It's a small gesture that can make a big impact on our mental health, and who doesn't deserve a little boost of self-love every once in a while?

Though this practice seems like a good idea at first glance, is there any hard evidence that it can make us happier as people? It turns out there is. A study headed by Christopher Cascio and his associates was published in 2015 in the journal *Social Cognitive and Affective Neuroscience*, sharing their findings about how self-affirmation affects the brain. They wanted to see if they could lift the hood and see what actually goes on in the brain when someone chooses to self-affirm.

They set up a study of sixty-seven participants who were then asked to rank the personal importance of eight separate areas of life. The areas were creativity, family and friends, humor, independence, business or earning money, politics, religious values, and spontaneity. Then, half of the participants were put in MRI machines and asked to think about the area of life they rated most highly. They were asked to dwell on these positive thoughts, visualizing themselves having related experiences, or thinking about the details of this area. The other half were not told to focus in this way.

The findings suggested that self-affirmation boosted activity in the ventral striatum and ventral medial cortex, which are areas of the brain connected with the experience of reward. What's more, the research also showed that when affirmations were future-based, they tended to have a more powerfully positive effect on the brain. An example of a future-based affirmation is: "I'm going to do well with my business next year."

We'll explore the way that thinking about the future can impact our happiness in the present in a later chapter in this book, but for now, it's interesting simply to note that words of affirmation are not mere words—they have real consequences on our neural connections and brain activity. Self-affirmations are not just fluff. The researchers claim that they act as a sort of psychological immune system or a modulator, buffering us against setbacks or disappointments by reminding us of the resources we have and the positive traits we still possess.

But the world of affirmations is more complex than it looks. It matters *how* we engage in affirmative self-talk. If we tell ourselves "I'm perfect just the way I am" but we don't really believe it, we could actually end up creating more psychological distress for ourselves. Instead, we need to pay close attention to the kind of affirmation we're giving ourselves. If we want to boost our feelings of self-worth and bolster our self-esteem, it may work better to draw attention to the things we value—for example, our work, hobbies, or relationships.

We need to remind ourselves consistently that our self-worth has a broad foundation, and by using affirmations, we can draw our focus to those things in life that we value and that give us purpose and meaning. But the researchers also discovered that these affirmations are turbo-charged when they are focused on the future. The theory is that if we can imagine a promising outcome, we can begin to create a version of ourselves that is better able to tackle any challenges that may come our way. Or, to put it as Cascio did, "We find novel evidence that a future frame may act synergistically with value-based self-affirmations to bolster a sense of self prior to threat exposure."

How can we use these findings to improve our own self-talk?

Importantly, it's about more than simply flattering yourself or saying nice things. To be value-based, affirmations of this kind need to remind you of the principles and beliefs you hold dear. The idea is that you can tap into your own integrity and identity, and this makes you feel your own worth and value more deeply. Which makes you happier!

Here are some examples of values-based self-affirmations:

- *I trust myself to get through any challenge that may come my way.*
- *No matter what happens, I can always choose kindness and compassion.*
- *I always speak up for the things I believe in.*
- *I'm a good artist who will continue to create the kind of things that matter to me.*
- *My family will always be there for me.*
- *I'm strong; I know how to use my talents to make money.*

Of course, yours might not look anything like this—values are always going to be unique and personal to the people who have them. But notice how each of the above are rooted not in a place of personal attributes or esteem, but rather in what we value as people. Notice also that many of them are oriented toward the future. Creativity, family, spirituality, money . . . what do *you* value? And how does that value look if you project it into the future?

In the past, self-help advocates suggested affirmations that focused on fixed, individual characteristics ("I am beautiful, I am successful, I am intelligent"), but it's easy to see why these can have mixed results. When you dig into your values, however, you are encouraging your brain to inoculate itself against future adversity, not to mention help you feel better in the moment.

To practice your own affirmations, simply make sure that each one speaks to your deeper principles and core beliefs, and then add a future element for extra potency. You can write these affirmations down and read through them throughout the day or say them every morning—in the same way as you would take a daily multivitamin!

The Reading Habit

It's hard to find any commendable person who doesn't claim that reading played a big part in their success. We all know that reading is an excellent way to learn, to broaden your horizons, to cultivate discipline, to spur your creativity, and even to connect empathically with others. Reading is great! But there also happens to be sound scientific evidence for reading as a habit that boosts your mental well-being, too.

When you read, magic can happen. You become engrossed in a whole new fictional world, with novel characters and a plot that pulls you in. A study from the University of Liverpool found that people who read experience lower stress levels than those who don't, not to mention they have higher self-esteem and psychological resilience.

Again, we can thank studies done using MRIs for our ability to examine the brain's activity during reading. When you read, your neural circuitry and networks are strengthened as you absorb yourself in the narrative. Humans really are built, it seems, for stories.

Another 2009 study by Mindlab International at the University of Sussex found that reading is associated with lower blood pressure, better sleep, improved mental acuity, less psychological distress, and better heart rate. They reported that just six minutes a day could reduce stress levels by sixty-eight percent. Cognitive neuropsychologist Dr. Lewis, who led the study, claims that "losing yourself in a book is the ultimate relaxation. This is particularly poignant in uncertain economic times when we are all craving a certain amount of escapism. It really doesn't matter what book you read, by losing yourself in a thoroughly engrossing book you can escape from the worries and stresses of the everyday world and spend a while exploring the domain of the author's imagination."

That's not all, though. In trying to understand the characters and the plot unfolding in the pages, our brains work hard to empathize and take on new perspectives, which in itself is a powerful way to boost happiness levels. Reading is like empathy and compassion gym! Reading literary fiction (i.e., stories that delve into the inner worlds of the characters) boosts our "theory of mind" ability, which is our capacity for imagining the mental worlds of others. This helps us become more empathic and intelligent communicators, which has effects on our real-world relationships.

A 2014 study in *Neuroreport* by Housten et al. shows how children who grew up reading books actually have brains that developed on completely different trajectories than those who didn't. The researchers found that reading shapes the growing brain in five different areas and can even increase overall brain volume. The more we read, the stronger the connections are between the neurons themselves and the different brain areas.

Reading has loads of other impressive benefits:

- Improves vocabulary and comprehension
- Boosts IQ
- Reduces stress level
- Counteracts anxiety and depression symptoms

- Reduces age-related cognitive decline
- Is just fun!

To conclude, reading is one of those daily habits that *indirectly* contributes to our overall happiness and well-being. When you sit down with a good book, you're not only distracting your mind from anxious or depressive thoughts, but you're also engaging in a form of self-care. Reading gives you the opportunity to escape from the chaos of daily life and immerse yourself in a world of imagination and creativity. Plus, you'll likely learn something new along the way, whether it's about a different culture or a new way of thinking. Because reading has such far-reaching benefits for health, cognitive abilities, and verbal/communication skills, it works in every area of life to make us more alert, responsive, empathetic, and overall more engaged with the world around us.

What should we be reading? Well, anything we like!

Try to get a little reading done every day, and build up to it if you're not quite used to it. Choose something you're genuinely excited to read about, but don't be afraid to mix it up and experiment with themes and authors you might not have considered before (remember the power of novelty?). There's been some suggestion that reading real books as opposed to tablets or devices is better (Lauren M. Singer, 2016, claimed that digital reading means lower comprehension), but pick what works best for you and find times throughout the day to squeeze in a few pages.

Blogs, graphic novels, news pieces, and long-form articles also count, but try to read them properly rather than just skimming and hurrying on to the next thing. If you can, try to focus intently on reading what's in front of you, somewhere quiet where you won't be distracted. This will help you cultivate discipline and focused attention. Finally, though reading in itself is a fantastic daily habit, you can boost its effects by choosing material that makes you happy. Read things that inspire, excite, or entertain you.

Dear Happiness...

Matthew Lieberman is a psychologist at UCLA, and his research has suggested that putting your difficult thoughts and feelings down in black and white can actually help you overcome them. He conducted a simple experiment where he asked volunteers to have brain scans and then afterward write in a journal or diary for twenty minutes a day for four days.

Half of the participants were asked to write about neutral experiences—just whatever they thought of. The other half were asked to write down their more emotional experiences, thoughts, and feelings. Then he scanned their brains again. Can you guess what he found?

Compared to those who wrote neutrally, the people who wrote down their emotions demonstrated greater brain activity in the area of the brain called the right ventrolateral prefrontal cortex. This area of the brain is concerned with emotional regulation, so the conclusion is that by writing feelings down, these participants were actually working to modulate and manage those experiences. Likewise, as the researchers investigating the meditators' brains found, there was also lowered activity in the amygdala, suggesting that journaling helped people manage the intensity of their negative emotions. Overall, this technique seemed to help people process emotions and downregulate stress and unhappiness.

"Writing seems to help the brain regulate emotion unintentionally. Whether it's writing things down in a diary, writing bad poetry, or making up song lyrics that should never be played on the radio, it seems to help people emotionally," Dr Lieberman said. Interestingly, Lieberman found that men seemed to benefit even more from this activity than women, perhaps because, for men, the act of expressing emotions abstractly is more of a novelty than it is for women. In any case, everyone can benefit from keeping a diary, and they don't necessarily have to discover great insights or come to any solutions or conclusions. Rather, the act of writing seems to help us externalize and make abstract our experience, which helps us manage and regulate it better.

If the idea of keeping a journal seems a little corny, don't worry, you can achieve the same benefits in other ways. The idea is simply to express and externalize your emotions in an abstract way, and you can do that with visual art, colors, music (maybe a playlist?), collages, doodling, short story writing, or even a messy combination of all of these.

Just remember to keep your diary private, especially if you're writing down very personal thoughts, and bear in mind that you are not trying to create a masterpiece to show off. Your diary doesn't have to make sense or be beautiful; it just needs to be a place where you can slow down, process, and put what's in your head down onto the page.

Try to journal every day if you can. You can purchase readymade journals or make your own. You can go for a line a day or fill up reams and reams of paper with "automatic" style writing. A great habit is to keep your journal next to your bed and scribble down your feelings before sleep—get your worries out of your head and down onto paper so they won't disturb your sleep!

Keep the Flame of Hope Burning

Have you ever noticed that when you have even just a tiny glimmer of hope, you feel a little bit better? Life can be tough sometimes. And in moments when stress feels like it's about to consume us, hope can be the light that leads us out of the tunnel. Keeping the flame of hope burning can work wonders on our mental and emotional health. It's like having a positive outlook that boosts our energy levels and puts us in a better mood. But what many don't know is that hope also helps to curb anxiety. When we hold on to hope, we create a sense of optimism that outweighs the fear and worries that trigger anxiety. And, as a bonus, that hopefulness increases our overall sense of happiness.

Therefore, hope really can be thought of as a consistent daily happiness habit. And it's something that absolutely affects our day-to-day well-being.

Have you ever heard of elderly couples where once one passes away, the other does, too, not long after? Ilan Wittstein is a cardiologist at Johns Hopkins School of Medicine and believes that you can, in fact, die of a broken heart. He and several of his research colleagues published an article where they identified "broken heart syndrome" or what they called "despondency." The team is not the first to be interested in this phenomenon. Other scientists have also noted a drastic increase in risk of death for mothers whose children have recently died, or a greater risk of heart attack or stroke for those who have been recently diagnosed with cancer. To put it simply, the darker the future looks, the worse our health in the present—i.e., hope can actually influence our longevity.

Before Wittstein coined "broken heart syndrome," another scientist, Curt Richter, conducted the frankly appalling rat experiments that proved just how powerful a force hope can be. In the 1950s, he put rats in jars of water and watched them drown, measuring the amount of time it took for them to give up swimming (yes, really).

Interestingly, most of the domesticated rats ended up paddling for days before succumbing to death. The wild rats (i.e., those who are renowned for their swimming ability) died within minutes of being in the water. The tame rats stayed alive for ages, but the fierce, wild, and independent ones died swiftly. Richter's theory was that the wild rats could not fall back on either fight or flight and could not help themselves. So, they gave up hope.

To test this, he took more wild rats, and shortly after he put them in the water, he pulled them out again for a little while before putting them back in. The result was that these rats learned that the situation was not, in fact, hopeless and—you guessed it—they continued to swim and fight for their lives. What we can learn from this experiment (other than the fact that some people are shockingly cruel to rats) is that when someone perceives a situation as doomed, they give up, but when they have a reason to keep going, they can and they do—often for a very long time. Richter simply discovered that "after elimination of hopelessness, the rats do not die."

Returning to the question of elderly couples, we can easily see that when one person no longer has "a reason to keep swimming," they could give up to such an extent that they, too, die. This admittedly morbid topic shows us that hope can have measurable effects, not just on our abstract feeling of well-being, but on our actual will to survive. The rats in the experiment were, for all intents, similar, physically speaking. But their will to live was almost completely determined by their own perception of whether they were doomed or not.

The conclusion for those of us who want to be happy is clear: Keep the flame of hope burning. Have something to look forward to in life. No matter what, do not allow yourself to think you're doomed. Remind yourself instead that even if things are hard, they can get better. If you are optimistically expecting a good outcome, it almost becomes a self-fulfilling prophecy because that hope allows you to tap into reserves of your own energy and willpower to make that good outcome happen.

Summary:

- Happiness can be tricky to define, but it all starts in the brain. We can turn to scientific peer-reviewed studies to learn the daily habits and mindsets most associated with well-being.
- Though routines are important, so is novelty; make efforts to mix things up now

and again and try something new every day.
- Gratitude is strongly associated with feelings of well-being. Say thank you, or simply dwell on all the things you have to be thankful for.
- Try meditation, but remember to approach it without grasping at goals or desired outcomes.
- Try self-affirmation, but focus on affirmations that are value-based rather than those dealing with your traits or performance as a person.
- Get into a reading habit to increase your empathy and communication skills as well as relaxation. Anything goes, but literary fiction is best for strengthening perspective and "theory of mind" ability.
- Journaling or keeping a diary can make you happier and help you modulate and regulate your emotions. Try whatever form works best for you.
- Finally, understand the role that hope plays in keeping people optimistic and resilient. Always have something to look forward to and you will discover you have endless sources of energy and enthusiasm to draw on. Don't give up!

Chapter 2: Quick Happiness Fixes

So, now that we've covered a few science-backed habits to build into your everyday routine, let's take a slightly different approach. Though habits can be powerful things, sometimes you just need a quick fix to step in and help you shake a bad mood. Life doesn't always go to plan, and sometimes it's worth having a "happiness toolkit" to whip out in an emergency situation.

If you are thinking "Well, my emergency coping mechanism is *food*," then you're actually not too far off the mark—more on that later. In this chapter, we'll look at a handful of practical tricks you can use in the spur of the moment to lift a low mood and brighten your day.

What Makes a Happy Song Happy?

Have you ever noticed how a happy song instantly lifts your mood? It's not just your imagination. Maybe you've also noticed that there are plenty of curated playlists out there (for example, on Spotify) that are organized specifically with the intention of making you feel energized, relaxed, or just plain happy. But how do people know which songs make them feel good? Can a song really boost someone's mood? Happy songs have been scientifically proven to boost your happiness levels and reduce anxiety (Scott, 2023). In fact, listening to uplifting music is an effective way to increase feelings of contentment and fulfillment. When we listen to music that we enjoy, our brains release dopamine, a feel-good chemical that helps us relax and feel happier overall.

It turns out that there are predictable characteristics of songs that people universally claim are happy. Neuroscientist Dr. Jacob Jolij at the University of Groningen set out to un-weave the rainbow and come up with a mathematical formula for a happy song, as well as the ultimate feel-good playlist. He began by closely analyzing the music of the British electronic band *Alba* and found that every single song was about a cheerful situation (or else fun, nonsense lyrics), was a little faster than the average song (an average of around 145 beats per minute—20 more than the average pop song), and was always written in a major key, which sounds peppy and confident.

These three elements, he would soon learn, play a big role in our perception of how "happy" a song sounds. While Jolij admits that a happy song is "highly personal and strongly depends on social context and personal associations," he still set about compiling his own mega-playlist of the world's happiest songs.

Now, it's important to note that Jolij didn't publish this research in peer-reviewed journals, but people seem to like his analysis anyway! If you're compiling your own playlist, take a page from his book and look for the three key elements, and then turn up the volume when you're feeling down! The songs were:

- "Don't Stop Me Now"—Queen
- "Dancing Queen"—ABBA
- "Good Vibrations"—The Beach Boys
- "Uptown Girl"—Billy Joel
- "Eye of the Tiger"—Survivor
- "I'm a Believer"—The Monkees

- "Girls Just Wanna Have Fun"—Cyndi Lauper
- "Living on a Prayer"—Bon Jovi
- "I Will Survive"—Gloria Gaynor
- "Walking on Sunshine"—Katrina and the Waves

Whether you agree with Jolij's taste or not, there's no doubt that music can completely transform your mood—and your life. In fact, science is also impressed with the effects that music seems to have on the human brain. A 2013 study from *The Neuro* by Salimpoor et al. has suggested that not only does music have profound and measurable effects on our brains, but that listening to novel music is especially satisfying.

Using (you guessed it) fMRI scans, participants were observed as they listened to songs they'd never heard before. Afterward, they were given the chance to buy the songs they'd heard and were asked to pay an amount they felt reflected their enjoyment. The researchers noticed that the brain's pleasure centers lit up when listening to new music (this is the nucleus accumbens plus other areas responsible for memory and emotion). Interestingly, the more activity there was in the mesolimbic striatal regions, the more that listeners were willing to spend on that music afterward. Salimpoor concluded that the strength of certain neural connections during listening to novel music predicted how much you would tend to like that music.

When you hear a really good song and you feel an incredible rush of good feelings, it's because your brain is literally awash in pleasurable neurochemicals as the dopamine reward system is activated—the same ancient system that activates when we anticipate sex, food, or the thrill of gambling. But the researchers also note that how much you like a new piece of music is heavily influenced by what you've liked in the past. "Depending on what styles you're used to—Eastern, Western, jazz, heavy metal, pop—all of these have very different rules they follow, and they're all implicitly recorded in your brain," Salimpoor says. "Whether you realize it or not, every time you're listening to music, you're constantly activating these templates that you have."

Professor Catherine Loveday is a cognitive neuroscientist at the University of Westminster, and she's been studying the way the brain processes emotions for years. Her findings echo Salimpoor's. When we listen to music we know and love, especially music from our past, we experience a boost in activity in the reward pathways in the brain.

The music we listen to during our teen years and early twenties has an especially powerful impact on our later memories because of what psychologists call a "reminiscence bump"—a period from about ten to thirty years old we are especially fond of reminiscing about. The elements of the music get tied—physically and conceptually—to our autobiographical memories and sense of self. So, when we listen to the music that was the soundtrack of a time in our lives when we were laying down the foundation of our identities, we may experience a particularly potent feeling of well-being. A little bit of nostalgia, in other words, can be a powerful coping mechanism!

When we return to potent emotional memories and events from our past, we are reconfirming our identities, reinvigorating ourselves, confirming our values, and connecting deeply to a time, place, and social group that we feel we belong to. On top of that, we get a satisfying dopamine hit that boosts our mood and may even strengthen our relationships and friendship groups. Salimpoor calls music an "intellectual reward" and an exercise for your entire brain, but it's also a very effective way to quickly shift how you feel.

Let's put all of this information together: How can we get the best out of music when it comes to increasing our well-being and happiness? The good news is that you're probably doing it to some degree already. Luckily, most of us now have access to all the music in the world and can easily find old favorites or endless new avenues to explore online. So, the next time you're feeling a little lethargic, sad, disappointed, or stressed out, use the magic of music to revisit old neural pathways of joy, connection, and meaning.

Create your own playlist for a dose of fortifying nostalgia and include all the "greatest hits" from your own history. This is not unlike value-based self-affirmations—you are tapping into a deeper sense of meaning, purpose, and value, only this time you're doing it in musical form. Choose songs that rev you up, make you feel hopeful and inspired, or just make you want to get up and dance. If you have warm and cherished memories around those songs, all the better. Maybe you choose a life-affirming song that reminds you of certain people you love and treasure—by listening to the song, you not only get a dopamine surge, but you also strengthen all that neural circuitry responsible for feelings of closeness, belonging, and gratitude.

But don't just stick to the songs you know. Add a little novelty to the mix and use music recommendation apps to suggest new music to you based on what you already like. Or, take a leap into the unknown and choose something new at random. Neuroscientists haven't yet figured out how ordinary people can magically induce certain brain states at will, but if they could, that magic would probably look like a pair of earphones and a few good songs!

Injecting Happiness

When it comes to happiness, there may be some wisdom to the "fake it till you make it" advice. Specifically, there is now research suggesting that a smile—even a fake one—can actually make you feel better. Yes, even a fake smile can trick your brain into thinking you're happy! Smiling sends a signal to your brain to release feel-good neurotransmitters like dopamine and serotonin, which can help boost your mood and reduce feelings of anxiety. But it's not just about faking it. Cultivating genuine happiness and fulfillment through smiling involves a deeper psychological shift, one that involves focusing on the positive in everyday situations and letting go of negative thoughts and emotions. So, the next time you're feeling anxious or down in the dumps, try smiling. It may feel awkward at first, but your brain will thank you for it.

The conventional understanding is that we smile because we are happy, but cognitive neuroscientists have suspected for years that it may also work the other way around—we feel happy because we are smiling. In other words, our facial expressions can influence our internal experience of emotions.

While most people know that Botox injections prevent the person from fully *expressing* their emotions, it turns out it also prevents them from experiencing those emotions themselves and recognizing and understanding the emotions of others. This makes sense—our facial expressions have evolved as part of our emotional and communicative makeup, and if our faces are frozen, it's likely others can't register, for example, that we feel surprised or angry.

The "feedback facial hypothesis," however, takes things a step further. One study in the journal *Emotion* (Davis et al., 2010) had half of the participants receive a facial filler that paralyzed the facial muscles, and the other half an injectable that didn't paralyze the muscles. Each group was then asked to watch movie clips and report their emotional responses. Those who had received the paralyzing Botox injections actually reported dampened responses compared to the other group.

What does this tell us? That our outward facial expressions and our inward emotional experiences are interrelated and that if we can't smile, we may actually not be able to feel happy. Subsequent studies have supported this idea that facial expressions are not just expressions of emotion—they are *regulators* of that emotion. This would explain why a study in the *Journal of Psychiatric Research* in 2012 (Wollmer et al.) found that subjects treated with Botox in key areas appeared to experience fewer depression symptoms—because they could no longer frown!

Researcher Justin Kim made a fascinating addition to this line of research. He and his colleagues investigated the effect of Botox treatment on a person's perception of emotional experience, and they were actually able to monitor this effect in the brain's amygdala, which is the brain's emotional center. Kim et al.'s research suggests that the amygdala is sensitive to facial feedback and that the ability to smile is a big part of expressing happiness, feeling that happiness, and understanding the happiness of others.

What does this mean for us? Well, it means we literally have a way to influence our amygdala and therefore our inner experience of happiness *from the outside in*—when we smile (even if we don't quite mean it) we are activating certain neural pathways and networks associated with happiness. When someone else smiles and we see their smile, register it, and reflect it back to them, we are participating in powerful nonverbal communication that can actually impact our mood for the better. Isn't that amazing? The look on someone else's face can have concrete effects on the electrical activity in your own brain! Even if you're feeling low, smile. Smile at others and you might be surprised just how easily you are "tricked" into actually feeling that happiness.

If you feel phony smiling when you don't feel happy, don't worry—research led by Dr. Fernando Marmolejo-Ramos at the University of South Australia found that faking it really does have real-world benefits. The research scenario went like this: Participants were asked to hold a pen between their teeth, which forces a kind of "covert smile," i.e., a fake one that nevertheless enlists all the muscles needed for a genuine smile.

Then, the participants were offered a range of stimuli, and their brains were observed. Again, the amygdala was seen to be influenced—when participants held the pen between their teeth, they reported more positive emotions, and this could be seen in their brain activity. What's more, the covert smile changed the way they perceived other people's facial expressions.

"When your muscles say you're happy, you're more likely to see the world around you in a positive way," said Marmolejo-Ramos. The activated smile muscles appeared to stimulate the amygdala, which then created positive emotional feeling states. It's as though our muscles are telling our brain, "You're happy. The thing you're perceiving right now is making you happy." If your muscles say you are happy, your brain believes it. So, our perception and our motor movements are blended together.

Does this mean, then, that frowning and scowling can make us feel bad in the same way? Possibly, although the research has yet to be done. But there's reason to believe that if you want to make yourself happier, it could be as simple as plastering a smile on your face and waiting for your brain to catch up! Knowing what we know about the brain's facial feedback systems, there are a few practical ways to bring more happiness into your life:

- When you talk to people, try to do it face to face rather than just via a phone call, since this way you can modulate your own emotional state by communicating nonverbally with them. It goes without saying that you should smile while doing so! If you're on the phone, smile anyway—you'll trick yourself into feeling happier, and this will show in your voice.
- "Smile at a stranger in the street" seems like slightly lame advice, but it could be a potent way to inject your day with some good vibes.
- If you're in the middle of an unpleasant task or feeling overwhelmed or bored, smile. You can convince yourself that your current adversity isn't all that bad after all.
- If you're feeling down, watch some silly videos or standup comedy and, even if you're not quite feeling it, push yourself to smile and laugh. Even if you're just laughing at yourself for being ridiculous, you're getting that amygdala working, and that's what matters!

Eat Ice Cream

Could it be that this book is giving you license to go ahead and guzzle ice cream to feel better? Well, yes. Yes, it is!

Picture this: It's a hot summer day and you're feeling a bit stressed out. Your mind is racing a million miles a minute, and you need something to calm you down and settle your nerves. That's where ice cream comes in. This beloved treat contains an amino acid called L-tryptophan, which can reduce nervous system activity. That's right, this natural tranquilizer is known for helping to reduce anxiety and promote sleepiness. Additionally, the sheer act of indulging in a delicious treat can be a mood booster in and of itself. But there's also some science behind it—eating ice cream can release endorphins in your brain that make you feel good. Plus, the cool and creamy sensation of ice cream can be quite soothing on a hot day. So next time you're feeling a bit anxious, don't hesitate to reach for a scoop (or two!) of your favorite flavor. It just might do wonders for your happiness, fulfillment, and contentment.

It's not just a tired movie cliché that unhappy people need an immediate dose of Ben and

Jerry's to lift a bad mood. It turns out that there's research to support the idea of ice cream as the ultimate comfort food. The Center for Neuroimaging Sciences conducted a study in 2010 to dig deep and understand why ice cream felt so, so good for those who were feeling bad. The researchers asked eight brave and selfless souls to eat ice cream while undergoing an fMRI scan. What they found was interesting: Eating the frozen dessert activated the orbitofrontal cortex, which is heavily implicated in the pleasure and reward circuitry of the brain. So, if after a bad day you feel a rush of soothing calm after eating a few mouthfuls of ice cream, now you know why: Your orbitofrontal cortex is releasing feel-good neurotransmitters.

Importantly, "ordinary food" doesn't seem to register the same response. This could be that ice cream has pleasant childhood memories and associations attached to it and is something we culturally consider a special treat. The psychodynamically oriented may even wonder if there's something more primally satisfying about ice cream, since it dimly recalls our very first and arguably most satisfying "comfort food"—breast milk.

You're probably wondering if eating ice cream every time you feel a little low is really such a smart idea. Isn't sugar and processed food bad for you? Well, yes. The research today is overwhelmingly in favor of a healthy diet for supporting well-being, and in this case, healthy means low in trans fats, sugar, and processed foods.

Epidemiologist Felice Jacka of Deakin University in Australia wanted to assess scientifically the effect of a good diet on mental health. In a 2017 study of sixty-seven participants, half were given nutritional guidance to improve their diet, while the other half were only given social support. After twelve weeks, the group with the improved diet guidance reported feeling happier than the other group. Dr. Jacka explained, "Whole (unprocessed) diets higher in plant foods, healthy forms of protein and fats are consistently associated with better mental health outcomes. These diets are also high in fiber, which is essential for gut microbiota. We're increasingly understanding that the gut is really the driver of health, including mental health, so keeping fiber intake high through the consumption of plant foods is very important."

A German study from the University of Konstanz found the same result—a diet high in plants led to higher overall happiness levels. Though other food categories influenced happiness, they consistently found that it was fruit and vegetables that contributed most to well-being. You've heard it before: A diet rich in fruits, vegetables, good fats, nuts, whole grains, and lean meats is the best for overall health and wellness.

So, what about our ice cream cure? Looking at the data available, it's likely best to consider ice cream a quick-fix happiness intervention, rather than a long-term approach. Though ice cream is delicious and a carrot won't pick you up after a breakup, consistently eating refined and sugary foods is likely to decrease happiness in the long run, not increase it. Also, since ice cream is one of those foods that most of us have registered as a pleasurable, special treat, part of the pleasure we derive from it probably comes from the fact that we don't eat it all that often. If ice cream isn't really your thing, and you have some other much-loved comfort food, the same rules apply.

Relive Happy Memories

We've already briefly encountered the power of nostalgia in the section on listening to familiar music, but what about simply taking a trip down memory lane? Could this make us feel happier?

Taking a stroll down memory lane can do wonders for our mental health. When we relive happy memories from our past, we tend to feel a sense of warmth and comfort. This is because nostalgia has the power to transport us to a time when life felt simpler and more carefree. When we feel anxious about the future, reminiscing about our past can remind us of our resilience and strength. Knowing that we have overcome challenges before and can do so again can also provide us with a sense of stability and security. Ultimately, nostalgia can help us feel more content and happier in the present moment.

Nostalgia often kicks into gear by accident—when we're reminded of the past by familiar sounds, smells, people, or situations. But what's happening in the brain when you reminisce?

Kentara Oba and colleagues published a research paper in *Social Cognitive and Affective Neuroscience* that looked at this very question. He wanted to know why exactly we feel so good when remembering things from the past. When we revisit "autobiographical events" from the past, the study concluded, we boost our psychological resilience. The team assembled a group of women and exposed them to nostalgia stimuli—i.e., visual cues to remind them of their childhoods. Then, they used fMRI scans to track what was going on in the brain. The researchers found that this reminiscing activity increased activation in areas associated both with memory and reward. These two areas of the brain appeared to be working together to create this unique experience we call nostalgia. They also found that the effect was somewhat individual and that certain individuals had stronger reactions to nostalgia than others.

Recalling memories tends to increase blood flow in the areas of the brain associated with emotion—the frontal, limbic, paralimbic, and midbrain. It really is as though we are living those emotional situations again.

But that's not all. The hippocampus, substantia nigra, ventral tegmental area, and ventral striatum are also activated, and these regions are associated with the brain's reward system. If you've ever heard a song from your past (a song that you don't even really like!) and felt a little pop of pleasure, it was likely because your brain's dopamine/reward system was activated. Of course, if the memories of this time were painful, it's a different story, but simply recalling places, people, or events from the past gives your brain a burst of recognition that registers as pleasurable.

Many people tend to get nostalgic without realizing that their memories are serving as a kind of coping mechanism and way to regulate negative feelings in the present. But we can also choose nostalgia deliberately as a way to alleviate the occasional low mood. We can look at old photos, go through a box of curios, listen to music from our childhood, flip through old journals, sniff smells we connect to the past, or recreate a dish that belongs in our personal history (this has double power if that food happens to be ice cream!).

But, remembering that nostalgia has concrete, measurable effects on the brain's release of dopamine, it stands to reason that we can become addicted to it in the same way we can with any other bad habit, like consuming junk food or alcohol. Like ice cream, it would seem that trips down memory lane are best when they're only occasional and not our predominant state of mind. Wishing away the present while yearning constantly for the past will naturally not make us happy but dismissive of and unappreciative of the present—where we actually live. But, if your nostalgia breaks leave you feeling warm and fuzzy and with more strength to carry on in the present, you're probably doing it right.

When it comes to memory and happiness, there is something else to consider: We can actively build new memories right now, in the present. If past memories are like a happiness inventory we can draw on when we're feeling down, then what about adding to that collection?

Meik Wiking is a prolific happiness author and the CEO of the Happiness Research Institute based in Denmark, and he's interested in the art of not just remembering happy memories but making them. He talks about, for instance, the fact that as we get older, we experience fewer and fewer "firsts," which makes life feel like it's moving faster and faster. But when we do something novel, we cement it in our memory, and it acts like an autobiographical touchstone in our history to return to. Wiking's first piece of advice for making memories is to choose deliberately to do something for the first time.

His second suggestion is to use the power of photographs. Like most people in the world, you probably have thousands of snaps on your smartphone, but Wiking recommends curating only one hundred (or choose a number you like) that represent the happiest moments of your life. If you can, print them out and put them in an album. Every time you flip through it, you give your brain a dose of dopamine and cement your autobiographical sense of self.

Another option is to keep your own private online photo journal and add a picture to it daily. Take inspiration from the many artists who take a snap of themselves every day—in ten years' time, they'll have an impressive collection to look back on. You could do this not only with photos but any image. Create a scrapbook of maps associated with special places in your history (for example, a couple can keep a book documenting the places of their first kiss, proposal, wedding, first home, etc.).

Make a visit to your old hometown—and bring a family member with you!—or keep curios and knickknacks from memorable trips. Keep symbolic items that remind you of noteworthy firsts or special moments—the first dollar you earned, a gift from a now-deceased grandparent, or a prize you won for poetry in the third grade, for example. As you identify these items or mark a special occasion, literally take a moment to pause and notice what is happening. Take an emotional and mental "snapshot" of the moment and imagine yourself filing it away for later.

Life can sometimes get routine and automatic, but if we take the time to bring in the extraordinary, the new, and the wonderful in small ways, time will feel as though it slows down. Try to make even insignificant occasions a little more special, and as you do so, draw on all five senses to etch the memory in your mind more deeply. Scent especially is a powerful memory trigger because it is closest anatomically to the amygdala and other memory centers in the brain. This explains the feeling of a certain smell carrying you straight back to a moment in the past, seemingly without your conscious or verbal brain being involved! Why not wear a new scent on every holiday as a kind of olfactory keepsake? Smelling that scent will forever act as a pathway to that memory.

Ultimately, creating new memories is all about attention. We cannot embed certain sensory experiences in our memories unless we have paid attention to them first. This means that if you want to create better quality memories, it's worth deliberately removing certain distractions and attention-hoggers from your life: i.e., endless smartphone notifications, ads, and unnecessary texts. Instead, streamline your digital life and be a little more discerning with the media you surround yourself with. Choose to be engaged with what matters to you; the more you focus on the meaningful things, the more meaningful they will feel. If you ask people at the end of life what they most remember, its usually moments of joy and connection with loved ones.

Every time you notice a little moment of this kind, it becomes one pixel in a bigger picture. And if those pixels are deliberately selected for their happy feelings, the overall picture becomes one of happiness, too. Famed cognitive research psychologist Daniel Kahneman has noticed what he calls the peak-end effect—i.e., our memories have nothing to do with the overall or average emotional experience but to the extreme point and the end point. For example, when remembering your wedding day, you may be inclined to remember the peaks (one specific moment during the vows) and the end (the memory of driving away from the party at the end of the night, thinking, "What a day that was!").

Sometimes, what we remember as a peak moment is not always pleasant. A moment of struggle can still be remembered fondly. The entire wedding could fade in your memory, but you never forget the thunderstorm the day began with or the moment your drunk uncle accidentally sat down on a slice of wedding cake.

In the end, if we wish to make better memories and boost our own well-being, we need to understand that memories are not *things*—they're *processes*. A memory is a neural pathway and a mental reconstruction rather than a fixed record stored in pristine condition in the filing cabinet of your mind. Take active control of your memory-making and memory-retrieving abilities and realize that memory helps you piece together who you are in the present. One day, perhaps, your life will flash before your eyes. The movie that will play in your mind's eye is one you are directing right now!

EFT Tapping

Donna Bach and fellow researchers published a paper in 2019 in the *Journal of Evidence-Based Integrative Medicine* called "Clinical EFT (Emotional Freedom Techniques) Improves Multiple Physiological Markers of Health." In this paper, they share evidence that the Emotional Freedom Technique, or EFT, may help reduce depression and anxiety and increase feelings of well-being.

In their experiment, they asked 203 study subjects to complete a battery of psychological tests before and after an EFT intervention to see what, if any, effect the intervention had. They also followed up on their results one year later. The findings were impressive: There was an increase in happiness by thirty-one percent, a reduction of depression by thirty-five percent, and a reduction in anxiety by forty percent. The team even noted some physiological improvements in things like blood pressure and cortisol levels—and the effects did appear stable after one year.

So, what is EFT, anyway? Gary Craig is credited as the founder of this modality, which is a kind of "energy psychology" based on the principle that thoughts and feelings are actually forms of "energy." Granted, this approach is not mainstream, and the research supporting it (over one hundred studies to date) is not perfect, but EFT is growing in popularity because people are interested in more straightforward, natural ways to improve their well-being.

In particular, the technique of EFT "tapping" has been acclaimed as a way to address a wide range of issues, from addiction to mood disorders to phobias. The great thing about EFT tapping is that you can practice the technique yourself with only a little training. The technique is something to use specifically when you're feeling stressed or if you encounter a particular psychological challenge. People have claimed to use EFT tapping before stressful or difficult events, for example.

Here are five simple steps to try EFT tapping for yourself.

Step 1: Zoom in on what the issue is.

You first need to identify what the problem is and what you're trying to achieve. It's best to focus on just one issue at a time. For example, you may have an upcoming presentation to deliver and are terrified of public speaking.

Step 2: Test initial intensity.

Look at the problem at hand and rank it on a scale of one to ten according to its emotional intensity. This is important so you can see the impact of the tapping and measure its effectiveness. Let's say you rank your pre-speech anxiety at around seven.

Step 3: Set yourself up.

Choose a simple reminding phrase that you will then repeat while physically tapping your "karate chop point"—find the outer part of your hand and tap at the fleshy middle point on this ridge. Your phrase is meant to note the problem you're facing but embed a sense of acceptance and acknowledgement despite it. For example, you can say "Even though I find public speaking difficult, I completely love and accept myself."

Step 4: Go through the sequence.

Now, you literally need to tap yourself on different parts of the body while you repeat this chosen phrase. This tapping can be done by an EFT practitioner or yourself. The order of tapped areas goes like this:

Top of the head

Beginning of the eyebrow (directly above and to the side of the nose)

Side of the eye (at the corner, on the bone)

Under the eye (around an inch below the pupil, again on the bone)

Under the nose (between nose and top lip)

On the chin (midway between lower lip and bottom of chin)

Start of the collarbone (where breastbone, collarbone, and first rib meet)

Under the arm (around four inches below the armpit, on the side of the body)

Two or more fingers are used to make the tapping movements, and the tap is repeated around five times on each area. Where you have two points (for example, one either side of the eye), you can tap one or both.

Step 5: Check the intensity.

Once you've completed the tapping sequence, check in to see how intense your feelings are now. You might find that your initial seven rating has gone down to a five or even lower. From this point, you can repeat the process until you hit an intensity of zero.

The process may seem a little bizarre for some, but if you are familiar with the principles behind acupuncture (also an energy medicine), this may not seem so strange. The great thing about the process is that it has a built-in baseline measurement that can help you see for yourself whether the tapping is working or not.

Donna Bach and her team are not the only ones to find encouraging evidence to support EFT. Morgan Clond published a 2016 systematic review of fourteen other studies and found that EFT does indeed help with anxiety. In the same year, Chatwin et al. compared the effects of EFT against another anxiety gold standard—cognitive behavioral therapy (CBT). Here, ten people underwent an eight-week program of either EFT or CBT. According to the authors, "both treatment approaches produced significant reductions in depressive symptoms, with the CBT group reporting a significant reduction postintervention, which was not maintained with time. The EFT group reported a delayed effect involving a significant reduction in symptoms at the three- and six-month follow-ups only."

In other words, CBT may be comparable with EFT, but more research will be needed. If you're thinking about trying EFT for yourself, it might be a good idea to seek out a practitioner first, just to show you the ropes. EFT has some support for certain conditions, especially anxiety-based problems, but the only way to find out if it works for you is to try it!

Flower Power

The old Chinese proverb tells us that if you only have two pennies left in the world, buy a loaf of bread with one and a lily with the other. It turns out that this advice is not just poetic, but it may actually be true: Flowers can literally feed the soul just as surely as bread feeds the body. If you've ever felt your mood soar after receiving flowers, or if you once smiled a little at a vase of daffodils in the window, there may be a scientific explanation.

Professor Jeanette Jones wanted to find out why the human brain feels so rewarded by the sight of colorful blooms. Her study had three categories: First, she wanted to understand the effect of flowers on women, then she wanted to know how flowers affected both men and women, and finally, she wanted to explore the affect they had on older people. Jones sent out ostensible thank-you gifts to 147 different women. Some were candles, some were fruit baskets, and some were flowers. Jones instructed the delivery men to act as observers.

When these observations were analyzed in a lab later, they confirmed what most of us probably already know: Flowers make women happy. In fact, they consistently produce a "Duchenne smile"—so-named after the researcher who first identified this genuine, unfakeable expression of happiness. But the men and elderly people who received flowers also showed a boost in their overall mood, as measured by their behavior and self-report. What's more, the effect lasted longer than the happiness produced in others by the candle or fruit basket gifts.

Jones published her findings in a 2005 paper in the journal *Evolutionary Psychology*. She concludes that "cultivated flowers are rewarding because they have evolved to rapidly induce positive emotion in humans, just as other plants have evolved to induce varying behavioral responses in a wide variety of species leading to the dispersal or propagation of the plants." Perhaps our ancient human history remembers flowers as a herald of spring and coming abundance after a long winter.

Who could argue with that? Despite having little value beside their aesthetic charms, flowers have been grown, arguably, for as long as humans have grown food. Flowers are a universal symbol of beauty, joy, abundance, and a gift that signals appreciation and love. They've been given as gifts to people all across the world for thousands of years, and many cultures have a system of communication attached to each bloom. But can our fascination with flowers be measured in the brain?

Another study by Lowri Dowthwaite, a lecturer in psychological interventions at the University of Central Lancashire, found that flowers can produce measurable bumps in people's dopamine, oxytocin, and serotonin levels, all of which create feelings of trust, bonding, well-being, and pleasure. Whether it's because of an ancient association of flowers with life and abundance, or flowers make us happy simply because they're pretty is still up for debate. But if you're feeling depressed, try flowers: Grow them, sniff them, gift them, or just buy a bunch for yourself and put them somewhere you can admire their simple beauty.

One beautiful example of how I personally utilize flowers to alleviate anxiety and enhance my overall happiness is through the creation of my own backyard flower garden. As someone who experiences occasional bouts of anxiety, I have discovered that immersing myself in the natural beauty and therapeutic aroma of flowers can be incredibly soothing and uplifting. Each morning, I take a stroll through my garden, carefully tending to each plant and marveling at the vibrant colors and delicate petals. The rhythmic process of nurturing and caring for these flowers helps me ground myself and find solace in the present moment. Witnessing the growth and blooming of each bud brings me a sense of accomplishment and joy, serving as a powerful reminder of the beauty and resilience of nature.

The act of gardening itself acts as a form of meditation, allowing me to focus on the task at hand and momentarily release any worries or stresses that may be weighing on my mind. This intimate connection with nature and the enchanting allure of the flowers fill my heart with a profound sense of calmness and serenity, creating a sanctuary where I can retreat and find respite from the pressures of daily life.

Summary:

- Though happiness is a habit, there are also plenty of immediate happiness "quick fixes" to use when you're feeling low and need something to pick you up.
- One great way to be happy is to use music. Pick songs that are relatively quick in tempo, written in a major key, and have positive and uplifting lyrics.
- You may find that nostalgic music from your past is especially good at summoning up good feelings.
- Studies done on the effect of Botox on people's ability to express and interpret facial expressions point to the interplay between our moods and our biology. Being able to mirror other people's expressions is important. Even though we think we smile because we're happy, we are also happy because we smile. This means we can often create good feelings by smiling—even if we don't quite feel it.
- Ice cream has been shown to be one of the greatest comfort foods that genuinely boosts mood, primarily because of its associations. A healthy diet is best in the

long term, but an occasional treat can be a legitimate pick-me-up.
- Recalling happy memories or making new ones has been shown to predict happy feelings.
- Finally, EFT tapping is an approach that can help you alleviate anxiety.

Chapter 3: Proven Happiness Methods and Techniques

We've covered a few happiness quick fixes, but in this chapter, we'll be looking at longer-term evidence-based approaches for building a happy life. These are things that we can do consistently, not only to cultivate strong positive feelings day-to-day, but also to prevent ourselves from getting overwhelmed by anxiety or depression.

The Happiness Behind Positive Anticipation

Have you ever noticed how often "hopelessness" is listed as a symptom of depression and how frequently unhappy people talk about having no future and nothing to look forward to? Or maybe you've noticed the opposite: that your mood instantly improves the moment you know you have an amazing vacation planned in a few weeks' time or a fun party happening tomorrow that you can't wait to attend. In fact, during the Covid-19 lockdowns, many people's mental health took a dip precisely because they no longer had any exciting plans waiting in their futures.

It turns out that anticipation of future events plays a big role in how we feel in the present. The human brain is built to look to the future because those ancestors who could better plan and prepare for what came next had a survival advantage over those who couldn't. It's what allowed our ancient ancestors to survive famines, winters, and unexpected adversities.

A 2005 study in *Cognitive Emotion* by Macleod and Conway showed that the more pleasant future events a person had to contemplate, the better their mood in the present—and vice versa. Whenever our brains anticipate some future reward, our entire state of mind seems to pep up in expectation of that reward, not to mention we seem to be better able to handle any adversity we face in the present.

We've spoken about the power of recalling pleasant events, like holidays, but it may be that *planning* such an event is half the fun. A 2020 paper in *Science Advances* by Igaya and colleagues identified a few noteworthy brain regions involved in positive anticipation: the ventromedial prefrontal cortex (associated with reward), the midbrain (connected to motivation and dopamine release), and the hippocampus (involved in memory creation and emotion). In fact, Igaya claimed that "anticipation can probably drive us to prepare better for actual reward consumption so that we can get the most out of it. It's also healthy—good for our mental health—to have something to look forward to, especially in a challenging situation like now. The reward is not physically here yet, but the brain somehow manages to create it in our mind."

Likewise, a study published in *Frontiers in Psychology* found further brain imaging evidence for how we process positive anticipation (Luo et al., 2017). In their experiment, the brains of forty study subjects were scanned while they performed an "emotion anticipation task" of either positive or neutral events to come. The bilateral medial prefrontal cortex was activated when people anticipated the positive outcomes—a state scientists have long understood reflects an overall sense of well-being.

Combining what we know about happiness and memory, we can see that the way we plan and schedule our lives has a powerful effect on our overall well-being. We could take the time to plan pleasurable activities in the future, both big and small, and then we can make sure that, as they happen, we pay deep, multisensory attention to what is unfolding. After the event is over, we can ensure that the benefit of those memories and good feelings are cemented in our brains by returning to the event and reminding ourselves what a good time we had. At the same time, we are busy anticipating the next pleasurable event on the horizon . . .

Let's be honest, the pandemic completely shattered many people's social lives and disrupted their vacations, their plans and hobbies, and their overall sense of fun. Though it may still be difficult to travel or make long-term plans, we can use the power of positive anticipation in other, more creative ways.

Remember, it is simply the act of planning and looking forward with hope that generates the warm fuzzies. You can do this by building in *mini*-plans and fun events in the future as often as possible. For example, make a plan to have something special for dinner the following evening, or fill up your calendar every Sunday evening with activities you know you'll enjoy—like a chat with a loved one or a trip to a store or park you like. If you've ever planned something like a wedding or a big party, you know that you can even derive satisfaction from planning to plan! Invite friends over for a chat, a drink, and a shared planning session where you put together details of a vacation—the anticipation of exploring new places, trying new foods, and relaxing in beautiful surroundings generates a feeling of euphoria that can last for weeks leading up to the trip. Even mundane plans like organizing a closet or scheduling a coffee date with a friend can bring a sense of purpose and pleasure to our lives.

This way, you get the happiness boost from socializing in general, along with the thrill of anticipating something fun in the future.

The classic "always have something to look forward to" advice turns out to be an excellent prescription for happiness. Try mixing up big events with many smaller ones and have a few long-term plans as well as ones you can expect to fulfill relatively soon. This way, your brain registers a rich, full life peppered with upcoming activities that will make you feel good. In a way, you are not unlike the rats placed in the jar of water—if you have something to look forward to, you have hope, and you also make it possible to endure whatever current adversities you face.

Take a Photo with Your Smartphone

Though there's been plenty of bad publicity about the effects that endless scrolling and social media have on our mental health, there's also reason to believe that smartphones can, in fact, boost happiness and reduce anxiety. Yu Chen, Gloria Mark, and Sanna Ali conducted an interesting study on this topic, the results of which they published in 2016 in *The Psychology of Well-being*.

They specifically wanted to know about the mental health effects of taking pictures with smartphones. They designed a four-week study including forty-one participants who were asked to take one photo every day depending on the research group they were in. The first group was required to take a smiling selfie, the second a photo of something that would make them happy, and the third a photo of something that would make someone else happy.

Can you guess the results? After three weeks of daily picture taking, the researchers measured the participants' overall moods and found increases in all three groups. They assessed overall well-being using, obviously, a smartphone self-report app that the participants checked in with three times a day. They also found something else: The selfie group noticed their smiles changing over time (getting more "real" and comfortable), the group photographing things they loved became more reflective, and the group taking pics of others claimed to feel more connection and intimacy with family and friends, and a corresponding reduction in their own stress levels.

"Our research showed that practicing exercises that can promote happiness via smartphone picture taking and sharing can lead to increased positive feelings for those who engage in it. This is particularly useful information for returning college students to be aware of, since they face many sources of pressure [. . .] The good news is that despite their susceptibility to strain, most college students constantly carry around a mobile device, which can be used for stress relief," claimed lead researcher Chen.

The three groups showed the researchers that smartphone photographs could be put to many different uses and that it could affect self-perception (selfie taking), self-efficacy (photographing loved things), or pro-sociality (photographing things for others' benefit).

In a way, what this research uncovered is not new: When we improve our self-perception, when we focus on what we value, and when we connect meaningfully with others, we tend to feel happier. What this study shows, however, is that smartphones and information technology in general can be a tool to help us achieve all this.

If you have a smartphone, then you, too, can try this for yourself. As you go about your normal routine, see if you can challenge yourself to take at least one picture a day—or three if you want to try one of each kind! Take a snap of yourself smiling in front of a pretty sunrise, photograph a piece of art you stumbled on that you love, or take a picture of something funny you know your best friend will appreciate.

Of course, we'd be remiss not to mention the fact that smartphones can also worsen your mood—steer clear of social media usage, especially if you notice that it's obviously making you feel inadequate, anxious, or obsessed! For some people, selfie taking can make them feel worse, not better. If this is the case, you may find that you get comparable happiness benefits without needing to use technology.

Unplug: Your Brain Needs a Break from Screens

On that note, it's worth mentioning that though technology *can* be used to increase our well-being, it's certainly not the only way we can create more happiness for ourselves. In fact, there are plenty of emerging studies showing the negative effects of too much screen time on the body, heart, and mind.

Gary Small is a professor of psychiatry at UCLA who has investigated both the positive and negative effects that technology can have on our well-being. Small has written more than five hundred scientific works and six popular books on brain health and well-being. His findings around screen time confirm what many of us suspect: Technology can be a double-edged sword. Things like video games, on the one hand, can relieve anxiety and boost our overall mood (more on that later), but nobody would argue that a nine-hour PlayStation marathon into the night signals anything other than addiction.

In an age when technology dominates almost every aspect of our lives, it's no surprise that our screen time has increased significantly. It's easy to get caught up in the endless scrolling, whether it's through social media or binging our favorite shows. However, research shows that excessive screen time can lead to increased anxiety levels (Khouja et al., 2019). Studies indicate that the blue light emitted from screens can disrupt circadian rhythms, affecting sleep quality and ultimately leading to more anxious thoughts and feelings. Furthermore, constant stimulation from screens can create a sense of always being "plugged in," leading to feelings of overwhelm and stress.

Excessive screen time—whether that's viewing TV, desktop computers, smartphones, or other devices—is generally associated with impairments to social, mental, emotional, and physical health. If you have children, you might have wondered if time on computers and smartphones damages your kid's normal, face-to-face communication skills—i.e., things like eye contact, empathy, and registering nonverbal cues.

Small claims, "Our research group recently found that sixth graders who spent five days at nature camp without even glancing at a smartphone, television, or any other screen were better at reading human emotions than sixth graders from the same school who continued to text, watch TV, and play video games for about four-and-a-half hours each day. The children who attended camp improved significantly in their ability to read facial emotions and other nonverbal cues to emotion, compared with the students who continued to use their electronic devices."

It's not a big leap to imagine, then, that those who have better social and communication skills end up being happier. This is, after all, precisely what the human brain evolved for in the first place. Most of us know intuitively that excessive screen time can't be good for us, but it really may be a question of both quality and quantity.

Taren Sanders and her colleagues published a paper in 2019 detailing the results of their study that investigated the behavior of over four thousand Australian children. The children were aged ten or eleven and were assessed at two-year intervals between 2010 and 2014. The researchers used time diaries to measure the children's screen time, which they then classed according to *type*: Screen time could be classed as passive, social, interactive, educational, or other. They also used various tests and metrics to assess the children's physical health, quality of life, emotional health, and school achievement.

They found, almost across the board, that the more screen time a child experienced, the worse their outcomes. But this depended on the type of screen time. Passive screen time was the worst, whereas educational screen time actually had some positive effects. So, the question "How much screen time is excessive?" can only be answered with "It depends."

According to Small, we have to balance our screen time with in-person contact with other human beings, but the Sanders et al. study also shows us that not all screen time is created equal. Sedentary viewing of TV is entirely passive, but the content may nevertheless be inspiring and uplifting, resulting in a better mood. Likewise, some games can be classed as educational, cooperative, and life-affirming, while others encourage compulsive, addictive engagement that isolates people from others. It's all a question of *how* we use the technological tools at our disposal.

Choose screen time that boosts happiness and well-being:

- Use apps and platforms to connect with loved ones.
- Consume media that teaches you something, inspires you, or helps you develop a hobby or skill.
- Notice how you feel after watching certain content, and avoid things that make you feel pessimistic, angry, or

anxious—even if they are technically educational!
- Before you sit down to stare at a screen, pause and become aware of what you're about to do and why. What is the purpose? Is it generally going to enrich your life in some way? Decide how long you'll engage, then stop after that period of time.

Appreciate Art . . . or Make Some Yourself

"Viewing art is like being in love." This is the conclusion not of a poet but of a neuroscientist who has investigated the phenomenon of art and its impact on our mental health and well-being. Semir Zeki is a professor of neurobiology and neuroaesthetics at University College London and claims that as far as the brain is concerned, appreciating art is not all that different from falling in love.

"There have been very significant new advances in our understanding of what happens in our brains when we look at works of art. We have recently found that when we look at things we consider to be beautiful, there is increased activity in the pleasure reward centers of the brain. Essentially, the feel-good centers are stimulated, similar to the states of love and desire," he says.

Again, we can thank the neurotransmitter dopamine and its work in the pleasure centers of our brains. In Zeki's study, around thirty participants were shown images of famous art while their brains were observed with an MRI scanner to see the resulting brain activity. The resulting patterns of activity closely resembled those of people who are in love—or using recreational drugs!

If you're wondering whether ugly or disturbing art has the same effect, the answer is no—the brain releases far less dopamine in reaction to these artworks. So, if you're not exactly thrilled by the art conventionally considered beautiful, then seek out art you *do* like—what is important is your subjective liking of the piece in front of you.

What's more, there is some evidence that creating art is also a mood-lifter, since creativity can boost your problem-solving ability, shift your perspective, and build feelings of pride and achievement. Art can make us more self-reflective, expressive, and contemplative—not to mention making it can be a lot of fun!

Creativity (yours or other people's) doesn't have to follow any particular rules or be too serious. Rather, it's about enjoyment. Today, artists all around the world are able to share their creations online more easily than ever before. And rest assured that art goes far beyond the stuffy oil painted "classics" you learned about in school. There is a whole world of different mediums, including digital techniques, not to mention people making art all across the world.

Bearing in mind what we know about novelty and surprise, try to find art that genuinely astonishes and engages you. Search out new images that speak to your emotions or impress you with their beauty, ingenuity, or strangeness. And if you feel the urge to create something yourself, don't censor it—making art can be an extremely effective way of regulating your own emotions and generating some positive feelings.

What *isn't* important is whether you're talented or not. Just like the goal of journaling is not to create a Pulitzer-winning novel, the goal of art for happiness is not to make something other people will praise. Rather, keep things open-ended and enjoyable.

One instance where I was genuinely astonished and engaged by a piece of art that spoke to my emotions and impressed me with its beauty, ingenuity, and strangeness was during a visit to a contemporary art gallery. Among the various exhibits, there was a large installation called "Transcendence" that immediately caught my attention. The artwork consisted of a suspended sculpture made entirely of recycled materials, including discarded electronics, metal scraps, and colorful plastic fragments. The intricate and unconventional arrangement of these materials created a visually stunning and otherworldly structure that seemed to defy gravity. As I stood beneath it, I was enveloped in a sense of wonder and awe.

The interplay of light and shadows, coupled with the unexpected combination of materials, evoked a range of emotions within me—a mix of curiosity, amazement, and a touch of melancholy as I contemplated the discarded items given new life. This artwork not only surprised me with its unconventional form but also resonated deeply with me, serving as a reminder of the beauty that can emerge from unexpected places. Inspired by this experience, I felt the urge to create something myself. Without censoring my ideas, I decided to experiment with mixed media, using recycled materials I had collected to construct a small sculpture. The act of creating without limitations or self-judgment became an incredibly therapeutic process. It allowed me to channel my emotions, express my own unique perspective, and generate positive feelings of accomplishment and self-expression.

Therefore, go to galleries to view art, and if you like, play around with your own creations to simulate all those in-love brain feelings. Failing all that, you can actually try to fall in love . . . but that's a different book!

Declutter

When Maria Kondo first began to gain popularity for her tidying up and organizational advice, it wasn't because people loved how neat and clean their houses looked using her methods. Rather, her success was all about how good people felt when they cleared up their living spaces. She subtitled her book, after all, "The *Life-changing Magic* of Tidying Up."

So, can tidying up really change your life? Can it make you happier?

Research does suggest that getting tidy and organized is an effective way to boost your mood, lower anxiety, and banish procrastination. It may be that *external* clutter somehow creates *internal* clutter, so when we clear up our outside mess, we experience a feeling of mental clearness, too. A UCLA study headed by Darby Saxby and Rena Repetti found that the presence of clutter (which they defined politely as a "high density of household objects") actually correlated with higher stress levels.

They assessed stress levels by measuring diurnal cortisol levels and discovered a definite link between how high this measurement was and the way that people (especially mothers) tended to talk about their homes. When they described their homes as chaotic and messy, they tended to have higher cortisol levels.

One reason could be that piles of items can represent a future (unpleasant) task and a constant reminder of what hasn't been accomplished yet. This affects self-esteem, too, making us feel guilty, embarrassed, or fatigued. We may be less able to focus because even though we are not really doing anything about it, our clutter still requires a certain amount of mental processing. One study even found that people with cluttered homes were more likely to eat unhealthily, move less, and be seventy-seven percent more likely to be overweight or obese. Peter Walsh's book *Lose the Clutter, Lose the Weight* expressly draws on this connection, showing how cortisol, clutter, and poor eating habits are all intertwined.

So, we can conclude that it's not so much that decluttering makes us happy but that living with clutter makes us unhappy. If we remove the clutter, we give ourselves a better chance of being happy (and healthy). If you find yourself guilty of living in a cluttered, messy, or chaotic home, then rest assured that there are only a few simple and practical steps standing between you and more positive, happy feelings about yourself and your home.

Step 1: Be honest about the clutter in your home.

Clutter will just keep reappearing if we don't address the emotional and behavioral causes behind it. It may be a good first step to be honest about *why* you have clutter, what it means to you, and what's standing in the way of getting rid of it.

Step 2: Start small.

If you get overwhelmed early on, your decluttering process will backfire as bad feelings make you want to quit or ignore the problem. Instead, set small tidying up goals so you can build your confidence slowly. Baby steps!

Step 3: Don't be a perfectionist about it.

You may be tempted to throw out your whole life and start fresh, but go slowly, be patient, and work through your clutter systematically, taking breaks if you need to. Solutions that work for others might not work for you. Just strive for minor, cumulative improvements rather than impressive quantum leaps.

It's a good idea to ask for help if you need it—these days, you can hire a professional decluttering expert!—and go easy on yourself. Also, spare a thought for more abstract forms of clutter. Take a good hard look at your daily routines and ask what can be streamlined and removed. Look at your digital habits and ask what is unnecessary and possibly stressing you out. We can even find "noise" and clutter in the media we consume and in our relationships.

Getting Rid of Digital Clutter: Notifications

One excellent way to improve your well-being? Declutter your notifications.

In the old days, the way we knew that someone wanted to get ahold of us was simple—the phone rang. Up until that moment, we were blissfully unaware of their intentions or their demands on us. We would need to wait until we were in the office to receive messages, and if we were out on the road or not at home, well, we were out of reach.

It seems like an inconceivable luxury in the modern world, but we can capture some of this earlier simplicity for ourselves. A study led by Martin Pielot and Luz Rello examined the experiences of thirty volunteers after they asked them to turn off their notifications. Every single participant claimed they felt less distraction and experienced greater productivity at work (yes, contrary to what your boss might say!).

The 2017 conference paper was titled "Productive, Anxious, Lonely: 24 Hours without Push Notifications." Participants were asked to disable all notification alerts across every device they owned for a full twenty-four hours as part of a "Do Not Disturb Challenge." Although people reported being less stressed after twenty-four hours, there was also a new problem.

"The evidence indicates that notifications have locked us in a dilemma: Without notifications, participants felt less distracted and more productive. But they also felt no longer able to be as responsive as expected, which made some participants anxious. And they felt less connected with one's social group. In contrast to previous reports, about two thirds of the participants expressed the intention to change how they manage notifications. Two years later, half of the participants are still following through with their plans," said the authors.

Again, we see that there aren't exactly easy answers when it comes to technology and the role it plays in our daily lives. If turning off notifications only makes us more stressed because we feel out of the loop and anticipate some kind of stressful catch-up phenomenon when we do plug back in, then obviously we need to make bigger changes to our lifestyles.

One way to tackle the question of technology and your own happiness is to try this challenge. Just view these twenty-four hours as a kind of check-in. See if you can set your smartphone aside completely and only come to it when you have some specific task in mind. Then, during that twenty-four-hour period, notice how often you feel compelled to reach for your phone—even if you have nothing in particular that you need to achieve. Sometimes, just grasping the extent of our automaticity and even addiction to smartphones can be a wake-up call. Only when we are not allowed to scratch this itch constantly do we get a real appreciation of how much it's affecting our lives.

If you find the twenty-four hours easy, congratulations! If you feel completely panicked and as though one of your limbs has been chopped off, it might be time to re-evaluate. Is your smartphone use really adding to your life? Or is it, on average, taking away from your happiness and well-being? Some people decide that what they'd really like to do is have a complete "digital detox" and get rid of not only harmful screen time and pointless phone notifications, but the bulk of their online behavior in general.

Remember the dopamine reward system in your brain? Well, clever scientists and software designers have worked very hard to create apps and tools that work on our brains in the same way that addictive drugs do. When we scroll mindlessly, the thing that keeps our fingers moving is the vague hope that something exciting might be forthcoming any minute now. When we see our phone flash or ping, our attention is instantly shattered as we turn to it to see if this might be something interesting. The human brain evolved to scan the environment for novelty—but in a world of constantly refreshing and artificial novelty, we are hooked by the very mechanisms that gave our ancestors a survival advantage.

Turning off notifications can leave us in a state of withdrawal for a while ("what am I missing?"), but some people find this diminishes with time. A digital detox gives your brain a chance to recalibrate and for your dopamine system to settle. You don't have to be a luddite forever, though. Just taking a break now and then can allow you to look at your digital habits with fresh eyes. Take, for example, the habit of the "infinite scroll" (or, to use the newly coined term, "doomscrolling").

Kaitlin Woolley and Marissa Sharif published a 2022 paper titled "Down a Rabbit Hole: How Prior Media Consumption Shapes Subsequent Media Consumption." They claim that the feeling of getting lost in media consumption and mindlessly scrolling for more happens because of "increased accessibility of the shared category: when a category is more accessible, people feel immersed in it and anticipate that future options within that category will be more enjoyable." The authors claim that similarity, repetition, and consecutiveness of prior media all impact how likely we are to keep scrolling and browsing, sometimes to such an extent that we're surprised by how much time has passed.

Their solution: reduce the similarity, repetitiveness, and relatedness of the content you're consuming. For example, avoid mindlessly clicking on "suggested" or "recommended" videos or articles (they're designed to pull you into rabbit holes), and if you watch or read something you enjoy, pause and digest it instead of immediately looking for identical content to reproduce that dopamine hit. Finally, if you find yourself engrossed in one activity (for example, reading the news), deliberately pause and switch to something else (for example, getting off your phone and doing something unrelated in the real world). This will make it far easier to loosen addictive tech's clutches on your brain's reward system!

Summary:

- There are several proven techniques for inducing happiness, one of them being the inclusion of positive anticipation in life, i.e., making sure you always plan something to look forward to in the future.
- Smartphones can drum up good feelings if you use them to take photos of yourself, something that interests you, or something that will make someone else happy.
- That said, your brain does need a break from screens, and a digital detox or notification-ban can help you relax and unplug, as well as cut down on distractions.
- Screen time is typically associated with negative outcomes, but not all screen time is created equal. Be conscious about the kind of media you consume and why,

choosing those things that make you feel better.
- Making or appreciating art is a great way to boost your mood, since it encourages a state of mind not dissimilar to falling in love.
- Declutter mess in your home and you may feel more relaxed and happier. Start small and don't put too much pressure on yourself.
- One way to declutter your digital world is to get rid of unnecessary notifications on your cell phone or other device.

Chapter 4: Creating a Happy Environment

As you're probably beginning to see, happiness is so hard to define because it takes on so many forms and has so many causes. We could imagine that a happy person is one who is healthy, content, and at home in their environment. And home is the focus of this chapter. In the same way that we can't expect a plant to grow without water, soil, and sunlight, it's a fair assumption that human beings cannot be happy in the wrong environment, either.

Though it may not seem like that big a deal, our immediate physical environments play an enormous role in our overall sense of well-being. If that weren't the case, big corporations wouldn't bother hiring specialist architects, designers, and industrial psychologists to make sure their workspaces were conducive to happy employees!

Green: The Shade of Happiness

Nature has always been an essential part of human life, from providing shelter and food to being a source of inspiration and relaxation. Science has proven that exposure to nature can have a significant positive impact on our mental health and well-being. Just a walk in the woods or a few hours spent in the park can lower our anxiety levels, calm us down, and increase our happiness and contentment. The fresh air, the gentle rustling of leaves, the chirping of birds, and the sight of greenery all work together to create a soothing and peaceful environment that helps us forget our worries and recharge our batteries.

According to a new paper by Dorita et al. published in the journal *NeuroImage*, viewing green spaces can help the brain improve attention and better regulate stress. Most of us won't be surprised to learn that exposure to nature lowers anxiety, calms us down, and makes us more content, but what's interesting about this research is that it identifies the reason why: the color green.

Plenty of research has been done on the humanity-healing benefits of green spaces, especially in urban areas. "Individuals exposed to green environments report lower levels of stress than those in less-green settings," say the authors. "In this work, we were interested in asking just how green environments engage the human brain, and how stress-regulatory benefits come about from exposure to these environments. It is one thing to show that all these environments are good for us—but it is just as important to understand why!"

The researchers did fMRI scans of forty-four participants' brains while they looked at images of streets, each with varying degrees of green foliage, grass, and trees. After a two-week period, the participants were asked to come back to the lab and give both their self-reported stress levels and their opinion on which pictures they liked best.

In those people who viewed the greener spaces, a very ancient part of the brain was activated—the posterior cingulate. This area in the limbic system is associated with motivation, emotion, and decision-making in the brain. It was via activation of this area that the researchers then observed that the participants' endocrine systems were better able to regulate stress.

This is an important finding: Walking in the forest or enjoying a beautiful garden is not just a nice thing to do; it has significant and measurable effects on our brains. The researchers are now interested in whether it's also the shape and structure of trees and plants themselves that have such a beneficial effect on us. City planners take findings like this very seriously, but as individuals, we can also do a lot to make sure there is more green power in our lives.

"We suspect that there is a relationship between the structure of green spaces and brain/mood/health responses, just as there may be in music. 'Mozart effect' experiments initially proposed that the complexity of Mozart was the reason for (temporarily) enhanced cognitive effects in young adults in solving spatial puzzles [. . .] The current understanding is that music stimulates the brain for clearer 3D and other complex forms of problem solving. So, is it the structure of the green (shapes of trees, variegation of texture and shade) or the prior-preference that induce the cognitive (and stress-moderating) effects?"

While they figure it out, the rest of us can look for more relaxing ways to bring a little greenery into our lives:

- Your brain evolved and took its shape in green environments. Re-create this by filling your home with potted plants (and flowers! See chapter 3 . . .) or giving your garden some TLC if you have one. It's possible that even artificial greenery could stimulate that part of your brain that registers natural spaces.
- If that sounds like too much work, consider occasional trips to garden centers or nurseries to get your fill of lovely green growing things, or else find a way to have a daily walk outside where you'll encounter plenty of trees and foliage. Even better, if you can punctuate your workday this way—you'll get in some healthy exercise, too.
- Color therapists (yes, it's a thing!) have long believed that the color green, which is smack bang in the middle of the visible light spectrum, is a balancing, calming, and peaceful color. You might find yourself relaxing more simply by having more of this hue around you. Wear green clothing, paint your home green, or enjoy artwork that incorporates a green palate or natural forest-y scenes.

You Feel Good When You Get Enough Zzz's

Nobody will be at all surprised to hear that sleep deprivation is associated with a worse mood. Missing out on sleep has easily measurable *physical* effects, but there is also plenty of research showing that it seriously interferes with working memory, decision-making ability, and attention spans. If you've had a bad day at work, feel grouchy, or find yourself a little "slower" than usual, poor sleep could be to blame—even if you don't feel especially tired.

The effects of not getting enough sleep go far beyond just feeling tired the next day and a decreased attention span. In fact, sleep plays an integral role in regulating our emotional states, and chronic sleep deprivation can have serious consequences for our mental health. One of the most common symptoms of not getting enough sleep is an increase in anxiety. In simple terms, when we don't sleep well, our brains become more sensitive to stress and less equipped to manage emotional reactions. This means that minor stressors can feel like major threats, leading to an overall sense of heightened anxiety.

One scary research finding (Matthew Walker, UC Berkeley and Harvard Medical School,

2011) suggests that because the brain is neuroplastic (i.e., it changes shape to adapt to whatever function it currently has), being consistently forced to work in suboptimal conditions may literally change it over time.

But surely we won't give ourselves brain damage by having just one late night, right? Sadly, it is possible. Andrea Goldstein at the Sleep and Neuroimaging Laboratory at the University of California, Berkeley says, "Our results suggest that just one night of sleep loss significantly alters the optimal functioning of this essential brain process."

Research led by both Walker and Goldstein used neuroimaging technology to investigate the relationship between lack of sleep and the way the brain processes emotions. What they discovered was that when a person was asleep, their brain showed increased activity in the regions of the brain associated with emotional regulation. While most of us can understand that sleep helps us regenerate and refresh on a physical level, what this research shows us is that sleep also helps "reset" and restore us emotionally, too.

If you've ever been sleep deprived and felt not only like a bus had hit you but also like you were ultra-cranky and ready to snap at the next person who breathed too loudly in your presence . . . well, this is why. Your brain simply did not get the chance to regulate and restore itself emotionally the night before. Sleep deprivation, the researchers concluded, interfered with emotional reactivity.

Naturally, getting enough good quality sleep affects every part of you, right down to a cellular level—your cognition, your immune system, your metabolism, and it turns out, your emotions. When we consider how much of our identity and sense of self stems from our emotional states, this becomes even more interesting. The researchers also suggested that sleep deprivation could result in us feeling less cautious and more confident in our decisions. You can imagine how this would influence the daily choices we make and our overall behavior at home and at work. If we are consistently overtired, we may start to feel that restlessness, irritability, and pessimism are actually part of our personalities.

The conclusion is obvious: When you're sleep deprived, it's much, much harder to be happy. Feeling well and content has a lot to do with how successfully we manage our internal state, i.e., our mastery of self-regulation. But if you're sleep deprived, all that self-control and awareness flies out the window, along with your mood.

The old advice still applies: Quantity-wise, get at least eight hours, and stay consistent with your waking and going to bed routine. Quality-wise, pay attention to your sleep environment and make sure you're giving your body a dark, comfortable, and quiet place to reboot every night.

Dogs, Cats, and Happiness

Most people will not argue with you if you define happiness as "a basketful of kittens."

So far, we've seen that we tend to make ourselves happier when we create environmental conditions that best mimic what our brains originally evolved to do. Dogs have been called man's best friend, and indeed this may be because dogs are the domesticated animal that we've shared most of our evolutionary history with.

Many, many people will attest to the life-affirming power of having pets (either dogs or cats—or both!), and most won't be exaggerating when they say how their four-legged friends have literally changed their lives. We all know that a friendly dog or a cuddly cat on our lap can make our day—there's no question about that—but now scientists can give us some insight into *why* pets make us so happy.

The journal *Frontiers of Psychology* published a recent paper (Beetz et al., 2012) examining the psychosocial and psychophysiological effects of having pets in your life. Their conclusion: it's oxytocin. The researchers combed through sixty-nine separate studies and compiled an impressive list of benefits, including lower stress, better empathy, improved learning ability, and even bolstered immune systems. Interacting with dogs and cats has been found in all these separate studies to correlate with improved social behavior and better interpersonal connections. It also improves blood pressure and heart rate, lowers biomarkers for stress and anxiety, and may even reduce pain.

They suggest that the "love hormone" oxytocin is behind all of these positive effects. When we cuddle and engage with our pets, we are stimulating the brain to release the same hormone that is released during childbirth, breastfeeding, and after sexual activity—i.e., it's the hormone that makes people want to snuggle, soothe one another, and show affection. The release of oxytocin has been credited with allowing us to feel in love, to feel safe and trusting, and to bond with others, usually via skin-to-skin contact and physical touch.

Beetz and colleagues also found that dog owners tended to experience greater mental health boosts compared to cat owners, probably because of the sense that loving a dog is in some way reciprocal—whereas cats are not ever one hundred percent domesticated and, though adorable, don't give the impression of needing humans in quite the same way dogs do.

Whatever the reason, owning pets can be one of the cutest forms of self-care, and those who have therapy dogs know this better than anyone. There are other benefits of pet ownership that, although not scientifically documented, will be loudly attested to by any loving pet owner:

- Pets can keep loneliness at bay, and they can keep those who live alone company.
- Taking responsibility for another creature's well-being can give shape to your routine and encourage you to stick to healthy habits—for example, getting up early every day to make sure the dog gets a walk. This responsibility can also give people a sense of meaning and purpose.
- Dogs and cats can teach us empathy and the power of building trusting, warm connections with others. The fact

that they don't speak our language is a plus because it teaches us to moderate our nonverbal communication skills! This can be especially beneficial for people who find social interactions with others challenging.
- Having a pet can make it easier to meet other people. Go for a walk with an adorable dog and you'll soon find that people are more interested in chatting with *you*, too.
- Animals can teach us so much about how to be happy. Most animals are kind, curious, uncomplicated, beautiful souls . . . and they never take life too seriously!

Of course, having a pet is a big responsibility, and nobody would recommend taking on an animal that you are not in the position to care for. If you cannot realistically own a pet right now, that doesn't mean you can't still experience the joys of what the researchers call "human-animal interaction." See if you can occasionally pet-sit for friends—some areas even have "borrow my dog" walking programs where you can help people by giving their dog a walk and help yourself by getting some exercise with an appreciative fur-baby.

Spend some time at the local dog park—greeting a few friendly dogs can do wonders to lift your mood. Or, consider volunteering at a dog or cat shelter where you can rest assured that not only are you doing something good for yourself but you're also helping those who most need it. Full-time pet ownership may not be an option for you, but you could offer your services as a temporary foster carer.

Now, if you were wondering if cat videos on YouTube counts as a human-animal interaction, well, the answer is a resounding yes!

A study in the journal *Computers and Human Behavior* claimed that as of 2014, there were almost twenty-six billion combined views on YouTube videos of cats, which numbered over two million. Clearly, the people watching must be getting something from the experience. The researcher team, headed by Dr. Jessica Gall Myrick at Indiana University, set out to discover what it was. They surveyed seven thousand participants who across the board reported elevated happiness and greater feelings of energy after viewing a cat video—this even extends to people watching these videos purely as a way to procrastinate. Apparently they felt more pleasure than guilt doing so.

Unlike eating your veggies or getting a workout in, this is one happiness prescription you're likely not going to have to force yourself to do. It turns out that getting a daily dose of "pet therapy" is as easy as watching a clip of a pair of fluffy kittens goofing around in a cardboard box. Just because the research concerns something cutesy and seemingly silly, it doesn't mean that its results aren't meaningful, especially in today's world, where depression and anxiety are on the rise.

If you're not doing so already, try to pause your work here and there to enjoy the simple pleasures of a cute or funny cat video (watching out, of course, that you don't get sucked into a rabbit hole! Videos of actual rabbits, however, are likely to be fine). If you already have a daily cat video habit and have a few favorite places you get your fix, then you can continue in the knowledge that you're not wasting time doing so—instead you're using the resources you have at hand to support your mental health. Well done to you!

One study led by James McNulty of Florida State University discovered that looking at cute cat videos could be good for your marriage. In the experiment, 144 couples (married less than five years) were asked to watch a curated stream of images three times a week for a duration of six weeks. For one group, these images combined pictures of the partner with cute animal pictures. For the other group, the partner pictures were simply paired with other neutral objects. The surprising result was that the former group reported greater satisfaction in their marriages than the latter.

A Japanese study led by Hiroshi Nittono found that looking at cat videos (okay, to be fair, it was *all* cute baby animals) correlated with better mood but also increased productivity when compared to those viewing boring old, non-fluffy, uncute neutral objects. The conclusion is clear: Whether you need a quick pick-me-up or a daily happiness fix that comes with literally zero downside, and whether you're at home or at work, consider watching a quick cat video or two. If your boss needs convincing, point them to the research—or just share the video with them.

A Quick Workout Can Turn Your Mood Around

Psychologists will often say that they already know the ultimate cure for depression and anxiety; it's just a question of convincing people to do it. That cure is exercise. A 2018 *Frontiers in Psychology* paper by Mandolesi et al. investigated the biological, cognitive, and psychological effects of exercise. The authors acknowledge that we already know that exercise is a powerful gene modulator (i.e., it influences which genes are expressed and which are "turned off") and that it can cause measurable physical changes in the brain, improving well-being. However, they were interested in the "hows" and "whys," so they reviewed a wide range of existing data, looking for patterns.

Their conclusions are unsurprising—via many separate but interrelated mechanisms, exercise improves well-being on several metrics:

Improved self-esteem and confidence
Better cognition
Lower risk of neurodegeneration
Better overall physical health
Improved sleep quality
Lower risk of stroke, diabetes, and obesity
Better emotional regulation
Reduced depression and anxiety symptoms
Improved longevity
Better executive function and IQ
Improved sex drive
Moderated effects of aging
 . . . and even better interpersonal relationships

It all adds up to a greater quality of life.

"Right now, the debate in the research world is over how *big* the benefits of exercise truly are, but those are just details," says psychologist Dr. Art Kramer, Ph.D. "What everyone agrees on at this point is that exercise has the ability to change your mood because it has a dramatic impact on your brain."

After just twenty minutes of aerobic exercise, your brain releases endorphins that can literally alter your brain's perception and stimulate the release of other feel-good hormones like dopamine. These effects are immediate, but they also linger for days, and when you exercise consistently, the real benefits start to accumulate as your brain literally changes in structure and function. One study (Liu and Nusslock, 2018) found that exercise literally encourages new neurons to grow in the hippocampus, which we already know is heavily implicated in emotions and mood regulation.

What exercise is best? The answer to that is: the exercise you most enjoy and are actually most likely to do!

All physical activity is beneficial for body and mind, but aim for around an hour a day, three times a week. Researchers at Bellarmine

University and Oregon State University (Loprinzi et al., 2011) found that exercise was a great way to relieve fatigue and increase sleep quality—but the ideal zone seemed to be 150 minutes per week.

One especially good idea is to cycle. There is now impressive evidence to support the idea that to feel better, you need to get on your bike, literally. Cycling is aerobic exercise that stimulates the release of dopamine, serotonin, and oxytocin. What makes it a good choice is that you can replace car-time with cycling. A 2014 study found that people who walked or biked to work were happier than those who drove. Actually, the longer you spent in a car, the worse your overall well-being!

Cycling is an especially good choice since it enlists all the major muscle groups, as well as boosts your heart rate, but without damaging your joints unnecessarily. Depending on where you live, it can be quite convenient and serve a practical purpose—getting from A to B. If you commute every day to work, you are squeezing in a workout while doing what you would need to do anyway. If you bike for leisure, you get to enjoy an adventure in the great outdoors and add a little socializing, too, if you go with friends or family. Why not get out there and explore your community a little more?

Of course, not everyone is going to enjoy cycling or want to invest in buying a bike. That's okay! At the very least, almost all of us can get up and go for a walk at any time without any special equipment or training necessary. Try hiking; yoga; dancing; Pilates; martial arts, including Tai Chi; swimming; rock climbing; athletics and gymnastics; jogging; weight training in a gym; long walks; or home workouts.

If you can, choose a regular activity that serves a few purposes, i.e., one that allows you to socialize, enjoy a hobby, or get outside in nature at the same time. For example, if you like the idea of swimming, why not join a wild swimming group in your area instead of coughing up money for a gym membership? This way, you get to enjoy nature and form a few friendships. In the same vein, combine a few happiness interventions into one by taking your dog with you on a jog or cycle, or combine the power of music, social connection, and movement by joining a spirited dance troupe. The more that you can weave exercise into your natural lifestyle, and the more you enjoy it, the more likely you are to keep returning to it.

Be Happy in Style

During lockdown, many people were thrilled at the prospect of being able to sit around at home in sweatpants and pajamas instead of dressing up to go to the office. A few months in, however, people began to understand the drawbacks of slovenliness. It turns out that the way we dress has a powerful effect on our mental state—and slobby loungewear doesn't exactly spell happiness.

Professor Karen Pine, researcher and author of *Mind What You Wear: The Psychology of Fashion*, has discovered that what women choose to wear each morning says a lot about her emotional state. Pine figured this out by asking one hundred women what they chose to wear when they felt depressed, and over fifty percent answered "jeans." On the other hand, when asked what they wore when feeling happy, only a third gave the same answer. Pine also discovered that almost sixty percent of women wear baggy tops when depressed, compared to two percent when feeling happy. Women were ten times as likely to wear a loved dress when happy than when depressed.

But if our clothing choices can reflect our emotions, can it go the other way around? Can we affect our emotional states by the clothing we choose?

Pine's study discovered that "happy" clothes were invariably well-cut, flattering, colorful, and made of beautiful quality fabrics. You'll notice that this description doesn't fit jeans! "Jeans don't look great on everyone. They are often poorly cut and badly fitting. Jeans can signal that the wearer hasn't bothered with their appearance," says Pine. "People who are depressed often lose interest in how they look and don't wish to stand out, so the correlation between depression and wearing jeans is understandable. Most importantly, this research suggests that we can dress for happiness, but that might mean ditching the jeans."

Enter the concept of "dopamine dressing." This 2022 trend has us all trying to find ways to perk up after a tough few years, and the fashion industry is on board, enthusiastically recommending color and playfulness. But is there any scientific evidence behind all this? Will wearing a dayglo-yellow shirt and funky trousers actually make you feel better about life?

According to Professor Pine, it's not that certain colors or styles in themselves are "happy" but rather that our associations and beliefs about them impact how we feel when we wear them. In a 2012 paper in the *Journal of Experimental Social Psychology*, Hajo and Galinsky introduce the term "enclothed cognition." According to them, enclothed cognition is about the complex set of influences that clothes have on a person's psychology and comes from both the symbolism we attach to our clothes, as well as what it physically feels like to wear them. To test their ideas, they did some experiments with, appropriately, white lab coats. They predicted that wearing this garment would increase people's attentiveness and care when doing tasks since they associate it with scientists and doctors.

The results confirmed their suspicions: When people were told the coat was a doctor's coat, they demonstrated better attention than if they were told it was a painter's smock. This means that not only did people have expectations and associations around the clothing they wore, but that this could literally alter the way their brains functioned, making them in this case more attentive.

Psychologist and coach Elizabeth Lombardo explains that "dopamine dressing" is not about specific colors or styles making us happier; rather, it's about optimizing the associations we personally make with the clothing we wear. She recommends keeping a clothing diary: "To begin with dopamine dressing, you should become more self-aware of your mood and dressing style. Maintaining a clothing diary is similar to keeping a food diary in that you should note which clothes make you feel the most comfortable and which outfits you like more in theory but never quite feel like yourself in."

Then, based on what you find, try to include more of these kinds of clothes into your wardrobe. If you're one of those people who feel *amazing* in a pair of jeans, then wear them. If bright colors make you feel foolish, don't feel like you need to wear them to induce a bright mood.

Look back on what you've worn this past week and ask:

Which items or outfits made me feel the best? What about them made me feel that way?

Which outfits made me feel the worst?

What pieces in my wardrobe are associated with happiness? How can I bring more of that into what I wear?

The Magic of Scented Candles

You've probably heard about aromatherapy before, but is there any scientific evidence for the effectiveness of nice smells as a way to boost mood? Research studies have been thin on the ground, but in a 2008 paper titled "Olfactory Influences on Mood and Autonomic, Endocrine and Immune Function," Kiecolt-Glaser et al. explore the effects that aromas can have on us.

Their study involved fifty-six men and women who were exposed to a range of scents both before and after a stressful stimulus (in this case a "cold presser") on three separate visits. The first odor was lavender (a relaxant), the second was lemon (a stimulant), and the third was actually a non-odor water control. The great thing about this experiment was that one half was done "blind"—i.e., the participants did not know which smell they were getting—and the other half were "primed"—i.e., told what smell was coming and what to expect from it. The experimenters themselves were blind.

After exposure to the scents, the participants were asked to give self-reports for their moods, and it was found that the lemon scent reliably boosted people's moods compared to lavender and plain water. It wasn't just the people's self-reports that showed a change, though. Several other biomarkers were recorded (for example, norepinephrine, IL-6 and IL-10 levels), showing that the lemon scent actually had made people feel better.

Psychotherapist Chryssa Chalkia has written about the effects of scents—in particular scented candles—on people's emotional state, and it's not hard to see why. Just like almost everything else we've encountered in the book so far, scented candles work by triggering the release of feel-good neurotransmitters in the brain, which then help with our emotional regulation.

And just as it is with dopamine dressing, it may be that scents are uniquely personal to the one smelling them. If you have happy and peaceful associations with the smell of cinnamon and orange peel because it reminds you of Christmas, for example, then this may be what you consider a "happy smell." Someone else may have decidedly unhappy associations around the idea of Christmas and actually find these scents cloying and claustrophobic.

Though a fancy scented candle in a pretty container is nice, you don't necessarily have to spend a lot of money to reap the olfactory benefits of aromatherapy in your own life. Opt for lemon-scented household cleaners or make your own with lemon essential oil. You could even decide to cook more with citrus or choose a personal fragrance that's heavy on zesty and fruity aromas, like bergamot, lime, or petitgrain. It may be that the simple act of lighting a candle and watching it flicker warmly in the corner is a cue to feeling happier!

Adjust Your Lighting

Consider just how often the way we speak about happiness involves metaphors of *light*. We associate mental clarity, well-being, and happiness with brightness, clearness, and sunniness—for obvious reasons. Depression, on the other hand, is almost exclusively a phenomenon associated with darkness, grayness, and lack of light.

Alison JingXu and Aparna A. Labroo of the University of Toronto Scarborough published a 2014 paper in the *Journal of Consumer Psychology*, where they explored the relationship between lighting and people's moods. Through a series of six different experiments, they found that people in brighter, more intense light actually experience more intense emotions.

Participants were asked to rate the spiciness of chicken wing sauce, the attractiveness of a person, their feelings about certain emotionally charged words, or how aggressive they felt a fictional character was. Throughout, they discovered that participants under bright light tended to answer all these questions with more intense emotionality. In bright light, it seems, everything is a little more extreme.

"Other evidence shows that on sunny days people are more optimistic about the stock market, report higher well-being and are more helpful, while extended exposure to dark, gloomy days can result in seasonal affective disorder," Xu said. "Contrary to these results, we found that on sunny days depression-prone people actually become more depressed," Xu claims, showing that it's not merely a question of bright equals happy and dark equals sad.

The team believes that their findings are explained by a deep human association between heat and light. They think that turning down the light turns down emotionality in general and deactivates the "hot emotional system." Turning it up doesn't necessarily make us *happier*, but it does intensify our overall emotional experience. "Bright light intensifies the initial emotional reaction we have to different kinds of stimulus, including products and people," says Xu.

The findings are intended to be used by marketers to influence the behavior of their customers, but we can make use of this insight. For one thing, the next time you need to be clear and levelheaded when making a decision, make sure you're not doing it in bright, blazing light. This may influence your perception in a bad way—you may be more reactive, more impulsive—in other words, more "hotheaded"!

But as far as the question of happiness goes, the findings do suggest that we can moderate our own emotional experience by tweaking the lighting around us. If you're feeling in a dark mood, double check that the problem is not that you're literally in a too-dark room. Get out there and get some vitamin D on your skin or invest in better quality light for inside your home. Good lighting is an art—seek the help of an interior designer to help you properly illuminate your space, or spend some time making sure that you're installing multiple light sources from each of the three lighting types: ambient (overhead or all-around lighting), task (to illuminate a particular activity), and accent (more decorative lighting that adds to the overall mood of a room).

Be careful—overly bright light is not a shortcut to happiness and may just exacerbate any unpleasant feeling you have. Instead, choose moderate, neutral lighting. Wherever you can, expose yourself to natural light. When you need to feel relaxed and low-key, turn the lights down low. When you need a burst of intensity, turn them up high.

Summary:

- A happy physical environment is a big part of maintaining well-being.
- Get outside and into green spaces, especially natural spaces filled with trees and foliage. Otherwise, try to surround yourself in the peaceful and happy color of nature: green.
- Make sure you're getting enough sleep (eight hours minimum) since the sleep-deprived brain is literally incapable of proper emotional regulation.
- Owning a pet can drastically increase your quality of life, but if that's not practical, find other ways to include furry friends into your day—and that means cat videos, too.
- Try dopamine dressing. There are no rules—simply be mindful about picking

items that symbolize joy and happiness for you personally.
- Scents can have a significant effect on our well-being; use scented candles in citrus scents to energize you, or opt for perfumes or cleaning products that you love the smell of or that remind you of happy memories.
- Finally, light your home strategically. Natural light is best, but you can create happy environments with artificial light, too. Studies show that intense light intensifies emotions. Turn down the lights when you need to make important decisions, but turn them up when energy and enthusiasm are flagging.

Chapter 5: The Social Side of Happiness

If you've read this far, you might have started to wonder: what about other people? Don't our friends, families, and partners play the biggest role in whether we're happy or not?

Well, they absolutely do. In this chapter, we'll be looking not only at the ways our relationships can influence our sense of well-being, but also ways that we can use communication and social interaction to boost our happiness levels.

Happiness Is a Call Away

Yes, it's always easier to reach out to people via email or text, but research from the University of Texas at Austin has found that a phone call might actually be the superior way to connect with others.

If you're one of those people who thinks phone calls are just too awkward to bother with, think again. Amit Kumar is a McCombs School of Business assistant professor and has co-authored a study with Nicholas Epley of the University of Chicago. The two published their research in the *Journal of Experimental Psychology*, where they shared that people actually experience more meaningful connection when they reach out in ways that allow them to hear one another's voices. This was despite their fear of it being awkward!

They asked two hundred participants to predict how it would go to contact an old friend, either by email or by phone call. They then randomly assigned each participant to do either an email or a phone call and asked them again to rate how the interaction went.

"When it came to actual experience, people reported they did form a significantly stronger bond with their old friend on the phone versus email, and they did not feel more awkward," Kumar said, which goes against people's predictions. Similar experiments were done where people were tasked with connecting via live chat, video chat, or audio alone (without video). The researchers discovered that people felt far more connected to one another when using their voices, even though they predicted it would be easier and more comfortable to text.

And to pre-empt the usual objection—the researchers also noted that conducting a phone call took no longer than writing or responding to an email. What makes this research interesting is that it directly addresses people's misconceptions while measuring the *actual* outcomes of certain behaviors.

Going deeper, it turns out that the power of the human voice can be explained by our old friend oxytocin. A paper by Seltzer, Ziegler, and Pollak titled "Social Vocalizations Can Release Oxytocin in Humans" explains just how important it is for our species to communicate vocally—that's what our voices evolved to do, after all!

Seltzer et al. already knew that physical touch could stimulate oxytocin's release, but what about simply hearing someone's voice? Could that have a similar effect? The team focused on mother-daughter pairs, assigning participants to one of three groups: complete contact, speech-only contact, or no contact at all.

They discovered that "children receiving a full complement of comfort including physical, vocal and non-verbal contact showed the highest levels of oxytocin and the swiftest return to baseline of a biological marker of stress (salivary cortisol), but a strikingly similar hormonal profile emerged in children comforted solely by their mother's voice. Our results suggest that vocalizations may be as important as touch to the neuroendocrine regulation of social bonding in our species."

What this means is that hearing another person's voice can be as beneficial to our well-being as having them physically present with us. Sure, it may *feel* like picking up the phone to call your mom is an awkward chore, but the science proves it—it's good for you and will make you happy!

Of course, it's worth noting the *content* of what you say when you speak to others, and your relationship to them. Social scientists and therapists have understood for a long time that isolation can be a killer and that one of the best buffers against mental illness is a robust social network filled with people you love. But it's not enough simply to have this network—you need to connect with them often to derive the full happiness benefits.

A study conducted by researchers Nicholas Christakis and James Fowler at Harvard Medical School found that happiness, though not literally contagious, nevertheless acts like a virus and can be transmitted from person to person. The study followed a whopping five thousand participants for a duration of twenty years and found that happiness can cause chain reactions throughout social networks. Happiness, then, is not a simple project one tackles as an individual but rather a collective phenomenon. The way you feel today, in other words, may have more to do with people you've never met than you thought! The social fabric you're enmeshed in matters.

The study found that when one individual was happy, a friend living within a mile actually experiences a twenty-five percent greater chance of also being happy. If you're happy, your spouse living with you has an eight percent increased chance of being the same, siblings fourteen percent, and next-door neighbors thirty-four percent. This effect could be traced for up to three degrees and can last up to a year. The closer people live to you, the more they are impacted by your happiness. In addition, people at the center of their networks demonstrate more happiness, likely because they're exposed to more happiness-inducing connections. Thankfully, the same patterns did not appear to be true of sadness, which doesn't seem to travel as well.

What can we glean from these results? It would appear that a major source of good feelings comes not from within us or from our individual behaviors, but from the company we keep. It stands to reason that we are influenced by our social networks most when we actually interface with others—at some point, we need to communicate and connect with people.

Now, if we know that communicating vocally and not just by text results in more satisfying connections (not just for you but presumably for the other person, too!), then it means that those separate connections are more meaningful and more happiness-generating. In the context of the bigger network, more quality connections mean more happiness to go around—and it does go around, since if someone in your network is happy, *you* are more likely to be happy, too.

Once, I found myself caught in the grips of overwhelming anxiety. Racing thoughts, a pounding heart, and a sense of unease consumed me. Desperate for some relief, I reached out to my best friend, Amy. As soon as she answered the phone, her voice poured into my ears like a balm for my troubled mind. The familiar timbre and gentle cadence instantly calmed my racing thoughts. It was as if her voice carried an invisible shield, shielding me from the storm of anxiety that had enveloped me.

With each word she spoke, I felt the weight of my worries slowly dissipating. Her genuine concern and empathetic tone provided a soothing presence, reminding me that I was not alone in my struggles. The sound of her voice, filled with warmth and understanding, wrapped around me like a comforting embrace, easing the tension that had knotted within me.

As we spoke, her voice carried a sense of familiarity and safety, creating a refuge from the chaos of my anxious thoughts. It became a lifeline, grounding me in the present moment and offering a sense of stability. Her words of encouragement and support acted as a guiding light, leading me away from the depths of anxiety and toward a place of calmness and reassurance.

In that moment, I realized the immense power of a familiar voice. Just hearing my best friend's voice had the remarkable ability to soothe my anxiety, as if her presence extended beyond the physical realm and into the depths of my troubled soul. It was a reminder that true friendship and genuine connection possess the extraordinary ability to provide solace, strength, and respite in the face of overwhelming anxiety. From that day forward, I held on to the knowledge that whenever anxiety reared its head, I had the unwavering support of my best friend's voice to guide me back to a place of serenity.

Therefore, the way to get some happiness is by going and spreading the love, not digitally but in person, or at least using voice, where you can both register a more complex, nuanced form of communication that no texting platform can recreate. When you're feeling good, reach out to others and share those happy vibes. If you're not, reaching out will make you feel happier anyway. This is not only good for you, but good for the world you live in.

Sing with Others

While we're on the subject of voices, let's take a look at some interesting research that suggests that singing has quite a few mental health benefits. People tend to think of the voice as an abstract quantity, but it isn't—it's more like a living, breathing part of your body.

Singing with others has been a powerful and effective way for me to reduce anxiety. There have been countless instances where I found myself feeling overwhelmed and burdened by anxious thoughts. However, in those moments, the opportunity to sing with others presented itself as a comforting and therapeutic outlet. Whether it was joining a choir, participating in a group sing-along, or simply harmonizing with friends, the act of singing together created an instant sense of connection and unity. As we raised our voices in harmony, a shared energy and collective spirit emerged, enveloping us in a safe and supportive space.

The power of singing with others lies in the synchronized breaths, shared melodies, and harmonious vibrations that resonate within us. Through this shared experience, I felt a profound release of tension and a deep sense of belonging. The music seemed to wash away my worries, allowing me to be fully present in the moment and immerse myself in the joy of creating music together.

Each note sang in unison carried a collective strength that transcended the anxieties that plagued my mind. The melodies weaved a tapestry of connection, bringing us closer together and fostering a sense of camaraderie. As we harmonized and blended our voices, I could feel the weight of anxiety gradually lifting, replaced by a renewed sense of calmness and inner peace.

The beauty of singing with others is that it encompasses both the physical act of vocalization and the emotional connection formed through shared expression. It provided an avenue for self-expression, allowing emotions to flow freely and be channeled into the music we created. The supportive environment, filled with understanding and acceptance, created a space where vulnerability could be embraced without judgment.

In these moments, I realized that singing with others not only reduced my anxiety, but it also allowed me to tap into a wellspring of joy, release, and authentic connection. It reminded me of the power of music to transcend the boundaries of individual experience and unite us in a common thread of humanity. So, whenever anxiety begins to weigh me down, I seek solace in the transformative power of singing with others. It is a source of healing, strength, and liberation—a reminder that in the harmonies we create together, we can find a refuge from anxiety and immerse ourselves in the transformative power of music.

Research conducted in Australia in 2008 by MacLean et al. did a simple survey on more than one thousand people that revealed something interesting: Choral singers reported an overall higher satisfaction with life than those who didn't sing with others. This effect remained even when the researchers noted that many of the choral singers faced more significant problems than average. And interestingly, the choral singers actually tended to be *less* healthy than average, with fifty-one percent of them having long-term health issues. What's more, they scored below average on a separate WHO scale of psychological health and social functioning. This is why it's so fascinating, then, that a full ninety-eight percent of them rated their own lives as good or excellent, and eighty-one percent said they were, in fact, satisfied or very satisfied with their health. Why?

According to Professor Don Stewart, head of public health at Griffith University in Queensland and study lead, "It's very much about the act of togetherness, the importance of being involved with others gives people this strong sense of connectedness and well-being."

While there have been suggestions that singing stimulates blood circulation and tones the lungs, we can see from Stewart's study that the effects of singing are *not* primarily physical but rather psychological. When we sing, we participate in the creation of music and boost our serotonin release. When we sing with *others*, the benefits are even greater. We stimulate the vagus nerve, which is the major nerve that connects brain and body. Vagus nerve stimulation paired with deeper, controlled breathing and co-regulation with others is a powerful cocktail for feeling good.

Co-regulation is important here. Consider what happens when you stand up with a group and do your best to sing along with them. First, you need to stand up tall, breathe deeply, and project your voice out into the world. This requires a degree of confidence. But you also need to match your efforts with others' and keep time with them. You connect nonverbally with them, watching facial expressions, working together as a group to modulate the shared sound you're creating—hopefully making something beautiful! As sound fills the room, you get a buzz—you're part of something. For this one moment, whether you're singing close harmonies or just belting out a pop song, you are in a tight community with others.

Seeing it this way, it's no surprise that group singing has had a significant place in every world culture and is deliberately included in celebrations, rituals, and moments of mourning. How can you take advantage of singing in your own life? First of all, don't worry about your voice not being good enough. Everyone can sing a little! There are plenty of choir groups out there that assemble for the sheer joy of it. Hunt them out and practice with them and see if you, too, feel your quality of life improving. If you're not quite ready for that, try karaoke with some good friends, or simply sing one of your favorites the next time you're in the shower.

Mix up Some Happiness in a Bowl

Happiness doesn't cost a lot and isn't difficult to achieve. It isn't mysterious and hard to get ahold of, either. Instead, many researchers are discovering that what makes most human beings happy are the simple things in life—the ordinary things we do every day. As it turns out, cooking is one of them.

When we cook or bake, we engage in a mindful activity that allows us to focus on the present moment and forget about our worries. The repetitive and soothing motions of measuring, mixing, and kneading can have a therapeutic effect on the mind and body. Moreover, the delicious aromas and flavors that emanate from the kitchen can stimulate our senses and increase the production of feel-good neurotransmitters like serotonin and dopamine. Cooking and baking can also be a creative outlet that allows us to express ourselves and feel a sense of accomplishment. Whether you whip up a batch of cookies, bake a loaf of bread, or prepare a gourmet meal, cooking and baking can provide a sense of comfort, satisfaction, and relaxation that can alleviate stress and improve our mental health.

Forget meditation or talk therapy; your next happiness boost may come from your kitchen. This is because, according to a University of Otago study published in *Journal of Positive Psychology*, little bursts of creativity work to improve our quality of life. And cooking is a form of creativity accessible to most of us. In this study, the researchers tracked 658 people over the course of a couple weeks and discovered that those who made time for small baking and cooking tasks reported feeling more enthusiastic about their lives. Studying their diary entries, these subjects were found to be thriving and experiencing personal growth.

A baking or cooking hobby could have cumulative effects that last long after the plate of cookies has been gobbled up. Dr. Tamlin

Conner, who headed the study, says, "Our earlier research found that positive affect appears to increase creativity during the same day, but our latest findings show that there is no cross-day effect. Rather, it is creative activity on the previous day that predicts well-being the next." If we can make a habit out of kitchen creativity, it may be that we create a kind of happiness momentum day after day. Which is a good thing because this is roughly how often we need to eat!

If you already are a kitchen veteran, you'll understand the therapeutic benefits firsthand. You feel in control, you focus on one small thing at a time, and being in the moment this way can almost feel meditative. Melanie Denyer is the founder of the Depressed Cake Shop in Los Angeles that explicitly draws the connection between feeling low and self-regulating with activities like baking. "Where there is cake, there is hope. And there is always cake," proclaims the website, which sells customized baked goods designed to raise awareness for mental health issues.

Interested in using the power of cooking and baking to boost your own well-being? Here are some ideas:

1. **Start small** and don't put too much pressure on yourself. Take it easy with a simple recipe that yields predictable results, then gradually work your way up to more complicated recipes as your confidence grows.

2. **Make cooking social.** You can invite others into the kitchen to help you create, or if you prefer to go it alone, make a point of sharing the love afterward by treating those around you to the delicious things you make.

3. **Stay healthy.** Heavily processed or sugary foods can obviously be bad for our health and therefore our psychological well-being. If you have an eating disorder or tend to overdose on sugar when given the chance, stick to cooking rather than baking. This is an empowering two-for-one: You enjoy the process of meal prep but also get to control the ingredients in a delicious, healthy meal.

4. **Mix it up!** Add variety wherever you can. Try new recipes, exotic

ingredients, or strange new combos. Challenge yourself to push the envelope sometimes—that's what creativity is, isn't it?

5. **Make it your own**. If you really can't be bothered to cook or bake, try some other creative kitchen pursuit, such as making jams or fermenting pickles. You may decide that what *really* makes you happy, on the other hand, is learning to master cocktails...

The PERMA Model

Martin Seligman is the brains behind the PERMA concept, which is a holistic model of well-being that outlines five building blocks of happiness. Let's dive in and see what they are:

- **P**ositive emotions—feeling happy and content
- **E**ngagement—being absorbed in what you're doing
- **R**elationships—warm and authentic connection with others
- **M**eaning—living a purposeful life
- **A**chievement—having a feeling of success and accomplishment

Let's consider each one in more detail. For Seligman, not all **positive emotions** are created equal. There is love, compassion, joy, pride, amusement, satisfaction . . . They're all different but all connected. Pleasure is connected to satisfaction of biological needs (like sleep or food), while enjoyment and delight have more of an element of intellectual stimulation—for example, the thrilling rush we feel after scaling a tall mountain.

As for **engagement**, Seligman is referring to that "flow state" feeling of being so engrossed in a task that you don't even sense time passing. This is a natural, attentive state that we don't typically associate with happiness but is actually there every time we are absorbed in a much-loved hobby, playing, making art, or concentrating on a fascinating puzzle.

As we've seen, **relationships** play a big role in our happiness—and this includes everything from a fleeting interaction to a lifelong friendship or marriage. Through our relationships, we learn to trust, connect, and self-regulate. We learn to communicate, we learn who we are as people, and we learn to cooperate and be part of something bigger than ourselves.

Speaking of which, **meaning**, says Seligman, is about having a purpose and direction in life, and this inevitably goes beyond temporary self-interest, money, or vanity. It's usually about going beyond the self and connecting to something more lasting, like a spiritual faith, a family, or service to some other higher value. There are as many ways to create meaning as there are people—things like volunteering, making art, or broadening knowledge all add depth and color to our existence.

Achievement refers to the attaining of goals (ideally those set according to our sense of meaning). We are happiest, according to Seligman, when we experience the pride and self-esteem boost that comes with setting targets for ourselves and then meeting them. Even if we don't achieve the goal, the mere fact of proactively and deliberately taking control of our efforts can make us feel more resilient and improve well-being.

So far, so good. But how can we put this descriptive framework to use in real life?

The PERMA model is really about reframing the way we think about happiness and well-being. Many of us have been unconsciously taught to seek our own contentment in ways that are guaranteed to fail. We might imagine that we will be happier if we lose weight, make more money, or craft a perfect, enviable lifestyle that looks how we think it should look. You only need to consider how often these approaches work to know that there is probably a better way.

What Seligman wants to show us is that happiness is not one single entity, one state of mind we can induce in ourselves in isolation. Rather, it's a result of many interlocking variables. So, we might feel happy one day because we are spending a fun day with our loved ones; this is about both engagement and relationships. But it's also about creating meaning, and after a day like that, we can feel a deeper sense of achievement and positive emotions.

In this special, happy day, there was no single action, thought, or feeling that is responsible for you being able to say, "I'm happy now." Rather, it was about all these pieces coming together. Thriving and living a life that is genuinely and not superficially happy goes beyond a simple "how to" list. The good life is one with many moving, interlocking parts.

"Positive psychology takes you through the countryside of pleasure and gratification, up into the high country of strength and virtue, and finally to the peaks of lasting fulfillment, meaning and purpose," says Seligman. Though there is so much to be gained from scientific research into isolated variables of human happiness, Seligman believes that a truly happy life is more like a work of art than a checklist of activities.

Seligman was inaugurated as the president of the American Psychological Association in 1998, and his aim was to shift the perspective from one of pathology to one of wellness. He didn't want to examine all the ways that human beings could go wrong; instead, he had the more classical question: what is a good and positive life? And how can we use psychology to help us create that life?

This is why he doesn't begin with a list of problems, with personal typologies, or with a diagnosis of why people are unhappy. Rather, he looks at what he believes are the five special ingredients for a life worth living. These building blocks can be measured independently, but they work together to create a whole bigger than the sum of the parts.

Just because the model has a more holistic focus, however, it doesn't mean there isn't robust scientific evidence to back it up. Research has shown that the PERMA components are strongly associated with better physical health and better life satisfaction. In fact, PERMA may be a better predictor of well-being than measures that only focus on what is lacking or distressing (Forgeard et al., 2011). This is why it's called "positive" psychology—because it focuses on strengths, possibilities, and thriving rather than the negatives of human experience.

If we want to make use of Seligman's insights in our own lives, then an important first step is to think in terms of *integration*. It is not merely the presence of each component that predicts happiness but the connections and interplay between them.

As you'll see, many of the suggestions for bolstering each component are ideas that have been independently verified by other research—and covered in this book. The trick to implementing them in real life, though, is to weave the activities into life in a meaningful, related, and joyful way.

For example, to generate positive feelings, you might sing, cook, enjoy music, go outdoors into nature, or get lost in a hobby. You could also jot down some notes in a gratitude journal or read something inspirational. All of these activities will feel good and put you in a contented, happy frame of mind. But have you ever tried some of these happiness suggestions only to find they don't really "stick"? Seligman's model can help us understand why: Though an activity may feel good in the moment, if the other components aren't in place, the activity won't tend to provide a deep, lasting sense of happiness.

This is why people with ingrained depression and anxiety get exasperated with what seems like flippant and superficial suggestions: "Just go outside for a jog! Have a smoothie!" Though it is true that exercise and better nutrition are associated with better well-being, these isolated interventions mean very little on their own. For example, you might have been told that being creative will boost your mood (and there is evidence to suggest it will), but in reality, you don't actually enjoy arts and crafts and have no talent in this area. So whenever you try, you zoom in on your shortcomings and create more anxiety for yourself. It's hard for you to be engaged or to find meaning. Maybe you also dislike the people at your art class, which means the relationship component is also not satisfied. So, there you are, participating in an evidence-based happiness activity that isn't making you happy!

Seligman would have a few suggestions here:

- Draw in your strengths, and this will help you become engaged. Choose

activities that are stimulating and provide a sense of satisfaction once mastered, but don't put too much pressure on yourself.
- Happiness is meant to feel good! Choose things you genuinely like.
- Tailor your approach to fit who you actually are. We should all be in nature more, but what does that look like for you? Beach or forest? Gentle stroll or extreme sports?
- It's important for every human to have genuine, loving social connections and support. But that may look different for each person, and your social needs may change over your lifetime. Joining groups and classes is a great idea, but don't discount the social network you already have—get in touch with an old friend or improve the relationships you already have.
- Set goals, but choose ones that genuinely align with your own values and skills.

Many of the suggestions in this book *do* work, but they have the best chance of working if they are expressed as part of something bigger and more meaningful—meaningful to *you*. As you read through these tips, then, consistently ask what your own values are and how (or if) you could apply the ideas in your own life.

For Seligman, human beings are complex, multifaceted creatures who experience happiness when their *whole life* reflects purpose, joy, connection, achievement, and pleasure. While there's a lot more to say about PERMA, a great place to start is to reframe your happiness project as one where you don't merely remove impediments that cause you suffering but cultivate all those virtues that help you *flourish*.

Drop Black-and-White Thinking

You've probably heard of CBT (cognitive behavioral therapy), but have you heard about DBT—dialectical behavior therapy? This is an evidence-based and highly effective therapeutic approach that has helped many with a range of psychological issues—especially interpersonal ones.

Let's begin with the word "dialectic," which in this context refers to a stabilizing conversation or a balance between opposites. Dialectical thinking is all about finding middle grounds and third possibilities, i.e., saying AND instead of OR or BUT. This counters a human tendency to think in black-and-white terms: Either we are happy or we aren't.

Either a person is good or they're bad. We've succeeded or we have failed.

It's this kind of rigid and inflexible thinking, though, that often causes and exacerbates personal unhappiness—not to mention that it tends to worsen communication with others and increase friction. If we learn to think dialectically, though, we can stop working in absolutes and stop *making* ourselves and others unhappier.

Let's say you're arguing with your family. Your sibling is angry at your parents for something they've done and is now angry that you appear to be taking their side and are not being supportive. A lot of the unhappiness and discord in this situation comes down to the black-and-white way it's framed: "You don't one hundred percent agree with me, so you must be completely on *their* side." You may feel put on the spot, having to choose a side, and your sibling may convince themselves to take your indecision personally.

This is a situation that could use some dialectical thinking! You'll know that you're in a similar situation if you find yourself using absolutist terms (always, never, everyone, nothing, completely, none, etc.) or feel pinned between just two potential options (there's no other choice—it's A or B; there is no C!). Here are a few principles of DBT that you can use, not just when you're feeling anxious or depressed, but whenever you need to clarify and improve communication in your relationships.

Be flexible. Rigid thinking means no wriggle room and no room for interpretation. But reality is seldom like this, and this kind of stubbornness actually makes us unhappy. There are few absolutes in life. If you are open-minded and flexible, you can stay aware of other possibilities and options and become aware of the things you're not currently aware of. In this example, we could bring in a little flexibility by slowing down and realizing that we don't *have to* choose a side. What other options are there? Do you have to act at all?

Find balance. Sometimes we accept situations for what they are; sometimes we go in and actively change them. Dialectical thinking allows us to find the balance between these two—which is a skill that requires we let go of all-or-nothing thinking. We don't have to be serene, all-accepting Zen monks bothered by nothing OR brave champions working hard to fix the world. We can accept some things *and* work at changing others. In this example, we can love and accept our sibling *and* feel unsure about their behavior.

Be patient. Some things take time to find their equilibrium. Imagine a ball dropped into a bowl—it rolls around before it settles evenly at the bottom, right at the center of the bowl. But it takes a while and a little back and forth. Sometimes, black-or-white thinking masks an impatience and anxiety that we need to hurry and make decisions. We may feel uncomfortable with ambiguity or unknowns, preferring an inaccurate conclusion over no conclusion at all. But really, we may just need time.

Try not to rush or force conclusions in yourself or others. In our example, this may mean you are able to take a step back from your family for a moment and realize that things may settle down on their own without you getting involved. Or, it may be that once you get a dialogue going, it takes a little back and forth before people resolve the tension and move on.

Using DBT in your own life is not about mastering techniques but cultivating a certain frame of mind. Try it for yourself and you'll find you are less rushed, less unhappy, and more in control. The next time you're feeling bad or are having issues in a relationship, pause a moment to ask yourself the following:

What information have I not considered yet?

Is there a third option?

Is it possible for me to wait, defer judgment, or say "I don't know"?

What portion of "the problem" is actually being caused by my perception and perspective?

What is the middle point between the two extremes of this situation?

Can I replace the "or" with an "and"?

Master the Art of Complaining

If we want to calm our raging anxiety and be happy, we'd better learn to shut up and stop complaining, right?

Maybe . . . but maybe not.

A 2015 study in the *European Journal of Work and Organizational Psychology* by Demerouti and Cropanzano tried to investigate the effects of complaining on mental health. The researchers asked half of their participants to write about a situation at work they were irritated by, and then they tracked the moods of these participants over the course of their workdays. They also had another non-complaining control group. The researchers discovered that the people who complained reported being less satisfied during the day—and even into the next morning—than those who didn't complain. Complaining, they concluded, does nothing to fix the problem and, in fact, just makes matters worse.

But could there be more to it than this? It's obvious that excessive complaining can damage our relationships and bring other people down, but few can argue that a good rant now and then isn't satisfying. The fact is, there will *always* be something annoying, unfair, or uncomfortable in life. We can't pretend it isn't there or lie and say that it doesn't bother us, so perhaps it's worth figuring out how to *complain properly*. In the book *The Squeaky Wheel*, Guy Winch explains the technique he calls the "complaint sandwich." This is a way to make complaints so that they actually help solve your problems rather than just exacerbate your bad feelings about those problems. Here's how to make the sandwich:

The first slice of bread is the "ear opener" to gently introduce your complaint to another person. The meat of the sandwich is the complaint itself. The other piece of bread is the "digestive," which helps the complaint go down better. For example, note the three parts in the following sandwich: "I'm very happy you've agreed to take on this project. You haven't followed the instructions for the first part, though. I'm sure it was just a mix-up, but if you could sort it out as soon as possible, I would really appreciate it."

You see, the problem with the way the people in Demerouti and Cropanzano's study complained was that it was *impotent*—the complaints never served any purpose and never went anywhere. But complaining can be put to good use if we approach it with either a solution or a very particular goal in mind.

Strategic complaining can actually be empowering if done correctly. You could complain about the weather to break the ice and make small talk with someone you don't know; you could complain to make sure others know not to take you for granted or try to wriggle out of responsibilities; you could complain to bring attention to unacceptable behavior.

Kowalski and colleagues published a study in the *Journal of Social Psychology* that asked the question, how do happy people complain? They concluded that happy (or more accurately, mindful) people tended to complain in a deliberate way and complained productively. The authors claim, "Perhaps people who are more mindful modulate the type of complaints they offer, preferring to engage in instrumental types of complaints over expressive complaints, thereby expressing complaints only when they believe they will accomplish desired outcomes."

So, how do we engage in more "instrumental complaining"?

One thing is to make sure that we don't dwell. Expressing unhappiness can be cathartic, can lower anxiety, and can get things moving. But if we *don't stop* complaining, we risk dwelling on those bad feelings and milking them for what they're worth. If you have something to whine about, put limits on it: Limit how long you will vent and who you will vent to. It's about moderation. It's seldom wise to complain excessively to someone you don't know well, so pick your audience wisely. Tell yourself that you're getting something off your chest, but after that, you will either take constructive action or you will keep quiet!

If something continues to bother you, use the energy of annoyance to power you to do something about it. If you cannot materially change your situation, then you could pick up your journal. But again, your intention counts. Instead of passively listing everything that's wrong in your life, use the written word as a way to process and release negative emotions rather than nurture them. Try to find some meaning or purpose in your annoyance, or use those pages to explore ways that you could cope and be more resilient.

Stop Counterfactual Thinking

Imagine that one day your boss gives you a ten percent raise. You'd be pretty happy, right? But if that same afternoon you find out that your boss also gave your colleague a fifteen percent raise, would you feel a little less happy?

Consider another scenario: Let's say that on that day, you were expecting to get a three percent raise from your boss (and actually got five percent), while your colleague was expecting to get a twenty percent raise (and only got fifteen percent). Who would be happier then?

We couldn't talk meaningfully about happiness, achievement, and social psychology without considering the fascinating phenomena around comparison, expectation, and competition. Again, we see that our happiness seldom emerges in a vacuum but rather emerges from our specific social context and the way we perceive our place in it.

Cornell University Psychologists Victoria Medvec and Thomas Gilovich and Scott Madey of the University of Toledo explain how the above scenarios are questions of counterfactual thinking. In essence, this is when we compare our achievements to what could have been or what we were expecting to happen. It's the human brain's ability to consider a "counterfactual" possible alternative world where things didn't go as they did. Whenever you say "if only" or "It could have been . . ." then you are using counterfactual thinking.

Counterfactual thinking can often increase anxiety. This is because when we focus on what could have been, we tend to dwell on the negative outcomes and become consumed by the regret of not choosing differently. This type of thinking can also lead to overthinking, where we constantly replay scenarios in our minds, causing us to feel anxious and stressed. Furthermore, counterfactual thinking can create unrealistic expectations for the future, making us feel as though we must make the perfect decision every time, leading to further anxiety and stress. It's important to recognize when we're engaging in counterfactual thinking and to try to shift our focus to the present moment, rather than dwelling on the past.

There was a clever way that the researchers decided to investigate this phenomenon: They closely examined footage of the awards ceremonies of the 1992 Olympics. They were interested in that moment when the winners and runners-up were announced and showed these scenes to undergraduate study participants, asking them to rate the winners' happiness on a scale of one to ten.

The results are strange: The silver medalists averaged a 4.8 score compared to the bronze medalists' 7.1. These scores actually dropped as the day went on, but the disparity remained. The third-place winners were happier than the second-place winners. Why?

More than ten years later, David Matsumoto and Bob Willingham were inspired to set up their own experiment and observed the facial expressions of eight-four athletes after Judo matches at the 2004 summer Olympics in Athens. Their findings: thirteen of fourteen gold medalists smiled after winning, along with eighteen of twenty-six bronze medalists. Astonishingly, none of the silver medalists smiled. In fact, they seemed positively miserable. While they were observed to smile later at the podium pose, these smiles were rated as more forced than genuine.

The results may be explained by the psychology of the athletes. They were not seeing their achievements in isolation but comparing them against their own expectations. *Both* the bronze medalists and silver medalists were engaging in counterfactual thinking—i.e., indulging in thoughts contrary to the facts. In the case of the bronze medalists, they may have thought "I could have finished in fourth place or worse, and I didn't!" which naturally makes their result seem like a lucky break to be grateful for. But the silver medalists were most likely to think "I could have won first place, and I didn't." This completely diminishes the result they did achieve.

What can we do with these findings when it comes to increasing our own happiness? Most of us won't have many opportunities to be ranked so obviously like these athletes, but it's still worth considering how our expectations color our perception. We may not even be aware that we are engaging in counterfactual thinking in the first place. We may work hard trying to reach some end point or achieve some goal, not quite realizing that we have already accomplished all the things that objectively make us happy—it is only our appraisal of that achievement that erases that happiness.

Most human achievements happen in context with others, and a little competition and comparison are inevitable. But maybe we can use this to our advantage. The Stoics are known for turning this phenomenon on its head: by engaging in "negative visualization," they deliberately contemplate all the ways that things could have been worse. This is not unlike cultivating gratitude.

The next time you're feeling low, forego the affirmations and instead think about how everything you're currently taking for granted could easily not have been there! It won't change your circumstances, but it almost certainly will change your appreciation of them.

Summary:

- Happiness doesn't occur in isolation but has a real social and relational aspect.
- Even though you may feel that you hate phone calls and prefer texting, connecting via voice is shown to make people far happier.
- Singing makes people happy, but singing together even more so. Join a choir if you can, and you'll feel happier about life—even if you're objectively less well off!
- Cooking and baking have impressive therapeutic benefits, and these can be

doubled if you cook with others or share what you make with loved ones.
- The PERMA model explains positive psychologist Dr. Selinger's five-factor framework for happiness: positive emotions, engagement, relationships, meaning, and achievement. Happiness is lasting when all five factors are drawn on and interconnected.
- Rather than ticking items off a list, happiness is about our unique strengths and values and what the good life looks like for us personally.
- Complaining is associated with unhappiness but not if we are selective and make sure to take action to solve our problems. The complaint sandwich can help others properly hear our concerns.
- Counterfactual thinking can alter our expectations and make us discount the achievements we've made. Instead of dwelling on everything you didn't achieve, try to focus on how things could have been worse!

Chapter 6: Your Brain and Happiness

People Get Happier as They Age

We'll begin with one common misconception: the idea that happiness belongs mostly to the young and spritely and that the older you get the more miserable you'll be. In fact, this assumption may be part of the reason so many people dread getting old. They imagine that beyond a certain age, people just have to settle down to a dreary routine and accept their slowly declining health.

But does the science have anything to say about happiness and aging?

It does! And it turns out that getting older can be an unexpected gift in the mental health department. There is research to suggest that older people are better able to perceive happiness and less reactive when it comes to fear and sadness—i.e., they really do "mellow"!

As individuals age, many tend to experience increased happiness and reduced anxiety. This can be attributed to a combination of factors such as personal growth, shifting priorities, and accumulated wisdom. For example, consider Mary, who is in her late sixties. Throughout her life, she faced various challenges and experienced moments of anxiety. However, as she entered her senior years, Mary developed a greater sense of self-acceptance and learned to prioritize her well-being. She decided to engage in activities that brought her joy, such as painting and spending quality time with loved ones. By focusing on her passions and nurturing meaningful connections, Mary found a deeper sense of contentment and serenity. Her accumulated life experiences and resilience helped her navigate difficult situations with less anxiety, ultimately leading to a happier and more fulfilling life.

Leanne Williams and colleagues at the Westmead Hospital in New South Wales in Australia asked 242 people between twelve and seventy-nine years old to view a series of photographs. These pictures were of people with different facial expressions. The participants were asked to select the photos that showed fear and happiness and distinguish them from those that showed sadness, anger, or disgust. As you can guess, their brains were monitored during this task using fMRI scans.

The results were published in the *Journal of Neuroscience* and showed that the older the people were, the more accurate they were at discerning happy expressions—in fact, teenagers were the best of all when it came to spotting fearful ones. The researchers noted that the medial prefrontal cortex showed more activation in elderly people than in teenagers—and considering that this region is associated with inhibition of the fearful responses of the amygdala, it stands to reason that older people are better at self-control and emotional regulation.

The part of the brain that deals with emotion control—called the medial prefrontal cortex—was more active in elderly people when they saw fearful faces than in younger people. This region has been shown to inhibit another brain area called the amygdala, which prompts fear.

Helen Fisher is an anthropologist at Rutgers University in New Jersey, and she thinks there's an important evolutionary aspect to this difference: "There would have been a tremendous advantage to have older people in the group with an optimistic view."

You may be wondering, though, if better emotional regulation is the same as being "happy."

Well, not directly. But if you are able to be less neurotic, less reactive, and better able to manage your own fears, it's reasonable to imagine that you would be more content with life. Exercising better judgment isn't something we usually associate with happiness, but if you're less bothered by things that happen, you will feel calmer and more in control. It's as though you can put the brakes on knee-jerk emotional responses and focus more on simplicity and improving your quality of life. In other words, your emotional maturity can develop with age.

The CDC published a study in 2004 showing that younger people (twenty to twenty-four years old) reported feeling down for an average of 3.4 days every month, whereas older people (sixty-five to seventy-four) claimed just over two days, and these results have been mirrored in other similar studies.

Harvard's Tal Ben-Shahar runs a course on Positive Psychology and claims that even if we're young, we, too, can cultivate emotional maturity by learning to tolerate and accept negative emotions and remember that happiness is "dependent on our state of mind, not on our status or the status of our bank account. Barring extreme circumstances, our level of well-being is determined by what we choose to focus on and by our interpretation of external events."

Play Video Games

While there are many reasons people enjoy video games, one potential benefit that often goes overlooked is their ability to lower anxiety and stress levels. When you're absorbed in a game, your mind is focused on the task at hand. This can create a sense of flow, a state where you lose track of time and become fully immersed in the experience. As a result, anxiety and stress can melt away, leaving you feeling more relaxed and at ease. Of course, not all video games are created equal, and some may be more effective at reducing anxiety than others.

We've seen the case against screen time, and we all know that gaming is supposed to be one of those guilty habits that falls in the same category as binge-watching Netflix reality shows or eating high fructose corn syrup. But even with this much-maligned hobby, there is a case to be made for the benefits of gaming.

Oxford University's Royal Society examined 3274 gamers who were defined as those who played either *Animal Crossing: New Horizons* or the iconic *Plants vs. Zombies.* These participants were quizzed on their game time and their overall mental well-being. The results were pretty straightforward: Those who enjoyed their gaming tended to report greater well-being than non-gamers.

However, you may have already noticed the catch: The kind of game you play matters. *Animal Crossing* has a notable social element that may be responsible for the happiness boost. Lead researcher professor Andrew Przybylski claimed, "If you play *Animal Crossing* for four hours a day every single day, you're likely to say you feel significantly happier than someone who doesn't," but he also added, "That doesn't mean *Animal Crossing* by itself makes you happy." They also claim in their paper that "need satisfaction and motivations during play did not interact with play time but were instead independently related to well-being."

In other words, it's not gaming, per se, but the enjoyment and sense of satisfaction that comes with gaming that boosts overall happiness. Remember the PERMA model that claimed that achievement and positive feelings were a key part of happiness? It may be that video games are simply one platform on which we can access a sense of accomplishment, pleasurable challenge, and some good feelings—not to mention a little socializing with a group that shares our interests.

Any gamer will tell you that not all games are created equal. There's no doubt that some games lack the elements known to enhance well-being, and others may be designed in ways that allow them to be subsumed into more addicted, compulsive, or unhealthy behavior patterns. So, does gaming make you happier? The ridiculous answer may be: "If it makes you happy, then yes."

Let's look at this example: Alex is feeling overwhelmed and anxious due to work-related stress. They decide to play video games as a way to relax and unwind.

Alex begins by choosing a calming game: They select "Stardew Valley," a popular farming simulation game known for its peaceful gameplay and relaxing atmosphere. The game allows players to cultivate their virtual farm, interact with friendly characters, and engage in various activities at their own pace. They proceed by creating a serene environment; Alex sets up a comfortable gaming space with soft lighting and plays soothing instrumental music in the background to create a calming atmosphere conducive to relaxation.

By focusing on the present moment, Alex essentially practices mindfulness as they immerse themselves in the game world. They pay attention to the intricate details of the pixel art, the soothing sounds of nature, and the gentle gameplay mechanics, allowing themselves to be fully absorbed in the calming experience.

They continue by setting reasonable goals: Instead of rushing to achieve specific objectives in the game, Alex sets simple, enjoyable goals for themselves. They might decide to plant and tend to a beautiful garden, interact with the in-game community, or explore the peaceful countryside. By focusing on these smaller, achievable goals, Alex experiences a sense of accomplishment and fulfillment without unnecessary pressure.

During gameplay, Alex takes regular breaks to stretch, hydrate, and rest their eyes. They use these moments to practice deep breathing exercises or gentle stretching to release any built-up tension in their body. Further, inviting a friend to join them in playing "Stardew Valley" multiplayer mode, they connect online and collaborate on various tasks, such as farming, fishing, or participating in in-game festivals. The social interaction and shared enjoyment of the game provide a sense of connection and reduce feelings of anxiety.

After each gaming session, Alex takes a few moments to reflect on the positive aspects of the experience. They focus on the relaxing moments, the joy of creative expression in the game, and the temporary escape from real-world stressors. This reflection allows them to savor the positive emotions and carry the sense of calm into their everyday life.

By following these steps and customizing their gaming experience to prioritize relaxation and self-care, Alex finds that playing "Stardew Valley" helps them reduce anxiety, unwind, and recharge their energy, ultimately contributing to a greater sense of calm and well-being.

You don't need to take up gaming if you don't already do it, since you can likely achieve the same results by doing any other fun or engaging activity (there's a world of games that are not digital!). If you do game take Alex's lead while also moderating your use so that you're engaging in something social that you genuinely enjoy. Obviously, if you find yourself compulsively drawn to a game you don't even enjoy that much, this is a red flag. The research only focused on innocuous "cute" games and didn't explore racing, shooting, or war games, so use your discretion if this is your chosen genre. Notice how you feel before and after a gaming session. If after gaming you feel riled up, pessimistic, or frustrated, it's probably best to look for a better game—or try a non-digital game!

Watch a Sad Movie

So, getting older might be something to look forward to, and long gaming sessions might not be bad for you after all. Perhaps one of the most surprising findings in the happiness niche, though, is that watching *sad* movies is associated with happier moods.

Watching sad movies can surprisingly result in happier moods and reduced anxiety for some individuals. This can be attributed to the cathartic experience and emotional release that sad movies provide, allowing viewers to connect with their own emotions and find relief. Additionally, the empathy and emotional connection formed with the characters' struggles can lead to a shift in perspective, fostering gratitude and diminishing personal anxieties. Engaging with the storytelling and narrative of sad movies offers a temporary escape from everyday stressors while also providing an opportunity to practice emotional regulation and coping skills.

Consider the example of Sarah, who has been feeling overwhelmed by work-related stress and personal challenges. In an attempt to find some solace, she decides to watch a sad movie one evening. As Sarah immerses herself in the film's storyline and connects with the characters' emotional journeys, she starts to experience a profound sense of empathy. The movie's depiction of loss, struggle, and resilience resonates with her own experiences. As the movie progresses, Sarah finds herself shedding tears, allowing a release of emotions that had been building up within her. The cathartic experience leaves her feeling lighter, as if a weight has been lifted off her shoulders. After the movie ends, Sarah notices a subtle shift in her mood. She feels a sense of emotional relief, clarity, and even a touch of gratitude for her own life's blessings. The sadness portrayed in the movie has paradoxically helped Sarah process her own emotions, offering a temporary respite from her anxieties and leaving her with a restored sense of inner calm and well-being.

A 2012 paper in the journal *Communications Research* was titled "Tragedy Viewers Count Their Blessings: Feeling Low on Fiction Leads to Feeling High on Life." In the study, 361 participants were made to watch a sad movie. But they were also asked before, after, and three times during viewing to self-rate on a series of metrics, like mood, inner thoughts, and overall life happiness. They were then asked to write about their thoughts on the movie.

The big surprise is that the sadder the movie, the higher these self-reports of happiness were. The conclusion head researcher Silvia Knobloch-Westerwick came to was that sad movies caused people to reflect on their own lives and their own relationships, and this heightened reflection led to a better appreciation of their own lives. In other words, observing someone else's tragedy seems to have the effect of bringing your attention to all the positives in your own life. This is not dissimilar from the technique of negative visualization or counterfactual thinking.

However, there was an important variable: Viewers who were prompted to think of their own relationships tended to get a happiness boost, whereas those who had only self-centered thoughts tended not to feel any happier. So, contrary to a popular interpretation, thinking "Thank God my life isn't as bad as those characters" isn't what makes you happier. The people who wrote about their own relationships after viewing the movie were the ones who tended to report being happiest after watching.

So, just as it appears with video games, it's not the sad movies that cause us to feel one way or another. Rather, it's the attitude we take to the sadness and how we interpret this. It was thinking reflectively about one's own situation that made all the difference—simply watching a tragic movie and feeling sad will not, on its own, provide any benefits!

We can think of the sad emotions such movies cause as a kind of stimulus, encouraging us to take a more appreciative look at our loves and what really matters. When we feel happy, there is no problem and nothing to look more closely at. But understandably, sad feelings may put us in a contemplative, problem-solving mood. We may look at our lives and realize how lucky we are and be reminded of what ultimately matters to us. In this way, even a movie with a terribly sad ending can feel therapeutic because it gets us in touch with ourselves and reminds us of the people we care most about.

If you're interested, the sad movie the researchers chose was the 2007 war drama *Atonement*, directed by Joe Wright—widely considered a tearjerker. Winning one Oscar and being nominated for six others, we can imagine that some of the appeal came from people's emotional engagement with the film. As an experiment, watch the film and see how you feel.

Dr. Paul J. Zak published an article in *Cerebum* exploring the way that "compelling narratives" (i.e., emotional, moving, or inspiring stories) actually trigger oxytocin release in the brain. This is the hormone that underlies feelings of connection and love, so understandably we may feel that compellingly sad movies touch us more deeply than comedies or action films. If you're one to cry during sad movies, Zak suggests that this is a good thing and means you're more likely to be empathetic and *better* at emotional self-regulation.

If you're feeling down, put on a sappy film and enjoy. *Schindler's List*, *The Notebook*, *My Girl*, *The Fault in our Stars*, or *Sophie's Choice* are all guaranteed to make you shed a tear or two . . . Once you're done watching, though, actively remind yourself of your own life and the people in it. Don't you just suddenly feel like calling up your mom and telling her how much you love her?

Buy Something New

Conventional wisdom tells us money can't buy happiness. But there are some more surprising findings to be explored, and one of them is that spending money can, in some ways, make you feel better.

University of Cambridge psychologist Sandra Matz and her research team did an in-depth analysis of six months' worth of transactions for 625 customers at a UK bank—that was over seventy-six thousand bank transactions. They grouped the transactions into fifty-nine different categories—for example, spending at garden centers, dentists, or coffee shops. Each of the categories was scored according to traits on the Big Five personality scale. As an example, charity spends might be highly associated with the traits of conscientiousness and agreeableness, and spending at nightclubs would correlate with extroversion. All 625 customers were given personality tests and asked separately to rank their satisfaction with life. Matz and her colleagues crunched the data and tried to see how well matched the spending habits were with the personalities of the people. For example, they noticed whether a person who measured as extroverted tended to spend on activities or items that aligned with that extroversion or not. Generally, they found that when people spend money according to their personalities, they reported better emotional responses and overall happiness afterward.

But what about other research that has found weak links—or no link at all—between consumption and happiness? In the 2016 paper, Matz concludes that "psychological fit" is the mediating variable. The research found that the better the fit between the product bought and the personality, the greater the happiness effect, and that this effect was more significant than a person's overall income or how much they spent.

So, money can't buy happiness—but buying things that align with your personality can . . . and this takes money!

Matz and colleagues did a follow-up study to confirm these findings. They asked different people to spend ten dollars, either at a bookstore or at a bar. They found that for introverts, spending at a bookstore increased their happiness, and for extroverts, spending at a bar increased theirs. However, when the spend was reversed, there was no increase in happiness.

"Finding the right products to maintain and enhance one's preferred lifestyle could turn out to be as important to well-being as finding the right job, the right neighborhood, or even the right friends and partners," says Matz. It turns out money does buy happiness—but it's not the absolute amount you have but rather how you spend it that matters.

It's about using money in a strategic, targeted, and deliberate way. Elizabeth Dunn claimed in her 2011 study on the subject that "most people don't know the basic scientific facts about happiness—about what brings it and what sustains it—and so they don't know how to use their money to acquire it." Her conclusion: if money isn't making you happy, then you're not spending it right!

Though most of us tend to shop by looking for the lowest price, Dunn claims we need to rethink this and consider the happiness we incur from the spend of each dollar. Her advice falls along key insights:

1. Spend money on experiences and not things (unless, of course, the thing enables the experience!).

2. Spend money to benefit others rather than yourself (yes, this really will make you happier).
3. Spend money on small things rather than big things (the happiness, it would appear, is equivalent).
4. Forget about spending money on extended warranties or complicated insurance—they won't make you the slightest bit happier!
5. If in doubt, delay spending or postpone consumption—you may decide in time that you don't really want something after all.
6. Avoid comparison shopping since it creates false urgencies and distorts your perception of value.
7. Focus ultimately on other people's happiness rather than your own.

Again, it would appear that our assumptions about how money and happiness relate are not often grounded in the reality of what makes us happy day to day. People may believe that owning a coveted gadget or expensive item may be the thing that makes them feel better despite consistent evidence that it is *sharing* and social participation that has the most reliable effects on our happiness. A 2013 study found that even experiences can fail to provide happiness if they're solitary—

it's when we include others that we seem to derive the most satisfaction out of an event or activity.

Imagine a scenario where Emily, a participant in the study mentioned, decides to go on a hiking trip to a beautiful scenic location. She plans to experience the serene natural surroundings and unwind from the stresses of daily life. In the beginning, Emily embarks on the hike alone, taking in the picturesque views and enjoying the tranquility. While the experience itself is pleasant, she notices a subtle feeling of something missing, a lack of true fulfillment.

Curious about the findings of the study, Emily decides to invite her close friends Sarah and John for a hiking adventure the following weekend. Together, they embark on the same hiking trail, sharing laughter, conversations, and the awe-inspiring scenery. As they make memories and experience the beauty of nature as a group, Emily notices a significant shift in her emotional state. The sense of satisfaction and happiness she derives from the activity is significantly heightened compared to her solitary hike. The collective experience enhances the enjoyment, deepens the connection with her friends, and creates a sense of shared fulfillment.

Through this real-life example, we can see how the study's findings hold true. While solitary experiences may provide some level of happiness, the inclusion of others amplifies the satisfaction derived from an event or activity. In this case, the shared experience of hiking with friends enriches the moment, highlighting the importance of social connections and meaningful interactions in enhancing overall happiness and fulfillment.

Recalling what we've already learned about the power of memory and anticipation and how important it is to cultivate happiness as a social and contextual phenomenon, this makes sense. Experiences can be talked about later or made into shared memories. On your deathbed, you're less likely to talk about a fancy watch you once bought than you are to fondly recall adventures, holidays, or fun experiences with loved ones.

If we consider, then, what the best spend of any sum of money is, we can probably derive the most happiness by focusing on what that money can help us *do* and with whom. Granted, there are gray areas. Splashing out on an expensive treat may create no extra happiness for us but incredible amounts of joy when we gift it to someone else. A TV may just be a TV for one person, but for another, it's a powerful tool that enables countless cozy nights shared with a loved one as they watch movies together (maybe sad ones?!).

This is why Sandra Matz's study came to the conclusion it did—there are no fixed rules for what counts as a "possession" and what counts as an "experience"—instead, it comes down to the degree of alignment between the money spent and what that individual values most in life. Remembering the PERMA model, we can see that anything that cultivates our feelings of achievement, meaning, or relationship to others will increase our well-being. So, buying a new sofa may not make you as happy as investing in a challenging but rewarding bike ride with your family, the people who matter most in your world.

Okay, so the lesson is to spend wisely and spend in accordance with your personality and values. Opt for (preferably shared) experiences if you want the most happiness bang for your buck. Finally, if you really want to make yourself happy, don't spend money on yourself at all.

In another 2008 study by Dunn and colleague Richard Norton, participants were given twenty dollars to spend on either themselves or on others, and then they checked in with them afterward to see how they were feeling. Even though the amount spent was the same, participants reported, on average, more happiness when they spent on others than when they spent on themselves.

Generosity, it seems, also benefits the giver—and the effects have been repeated in other studies done all over the world. Similar studies have tried to tease apart just exactly what mode of giving leads to the most happiness, and they find time and again that, dollar for dollar, "pro-social spending" has the highest returns happiness-wise.

And there could be a neural basis for it all. A University of Zurich study led by Soyoung Q. Park informed fifty participants that they would receive money in four weeks, before being split into two groups—one deciding to spend on themselves and the second to spend on others. Then, the participants were asked to perform a decision-making task while their brain activity was analyzed. The people who committed to spending on others actually showed differences in brain function, with more activity in areas associated with both generosity and happiness. Importantly, merely the *thought* of being generous had this effect.

There are some caveats, though. Some studies have shown that the happy feelings are exaggerated when the recipient is closer to you, which makes evolutionary sense. But it may also be down to the fact that when people are closer to home, we can see the effect that our generosity has on them, which turns out to be an important factor. Lara Ankin, who worked extensively with both Dunn and Norton, conducted research that found that people were happiest with their charitable donations when they could see and appreciate the effects they had.

There's one more interesting finding worth considering in the question of money and happiness. A 2002 study by Kasser and Sheldon discovered that the people who were happiest around the Christmas season were those who also put greater emphasis on the religious, traditional, and family aspects of the holiday and less on the consumption aspects. It would seem that people who value other things above money tend to have happier lives in general.

Let's put it all together: We cannot hope for material consumption and money to make us happier as people (despite everything the marketers would have us believe). On the other hand, money is a tool and, used correctly, can play a big role in helping us engage in the things that *do* make us happy—being with others, expressing ourselves, contributing to what matters, and living a life of meaning and purpose.

Prioritize Future Happiness, Prioritize Positivity

Now that most people are familiar with "living in the moment" and the power of mindfulness, it may come as a surprise that prioritizing future happiness has value, too.

When it comes to managing anxiety, prioritizing future happiness and positivity can make a big difference. By focusing on the positive aspects of life, such as relationships, hobbies, and personal goals, you can cultivate a sense of fulfillment and purpose that can help counteract feelings of worry or distress. Similarly, directing your attention toward the future can help you stay motivated and engaged in pursuing those long-term goals and aspirations that inspire you. By keeping your eyes firmly fixed on the horizon and prioritizing the things that bring you joy and fulfillment, you can create a sense of momentum and progress that can help to keep anxiety at bay.

Consider someone who finds happiness and contentment important things to aim for in life. Even when they do feel happy, they wonder if they should be feeling even happier. They may read a lot of self-help books or do their best to achieve some ideal state of mind, where everything, finally, is as it should be.

You can picture how such a person invariably makes themselves more unhappy. In fact, a study published in the journal *Emotion* found precisely this: When people overemphasize the project of being happy, they actually tend to worsen their mood. In other words, trying too hard can backfire and make you miserable.

Just like the silver medalists we considered in an earlier section, people striving for happiness may find that they frequently fall short. The study's authors say, "Valuing happiness could be self-defeating because the more people value happiness, the more likely they will feel disappointed. Paradoxically, therefore, valuing happiness may lead people to be less happy just when happiness is within reach."

It's a form of what is now understood to be "toxic positivity." The irony is that the more relentlessly we pursue happiness and well-being, the more intolerant we become to everything that seemingly doesn't fit the picture. We may become less adept at listening to others and empathizing and instead rush in to cheer them or look for a silver lining. Perhaps even worse, we become less able to acknowledge how we feel as people and deny, downplay, or ignore genuine negative feelings—meaning they never get processed or resolved.

A recent 2020 study by Humphrey et al. in *The Journal of Positive Psychology* identified two general orientations that people could have. They separated 496 people into these two groups: The first was people who prioritized happiness, and the second prioritized positivity. What's the difference? Those who valued happiness were more likely to agree with statements like "I believe I've failed in life if I'm depressed or anxious" and "I'm concerned about my happiness even when I feel happy." People who valued positivity, on the other hand, were more likely to agree with statements like "I notice and choose to nurture my positive emotions."

Comparing the groups, the researchers noticed that those who value happiness actually tend to feel it less often and have difficulty knowing what to do with negative emotions. Those who value positivity believe that negative emotions are just a part of life, and consequently, they don't feel like something is wrong when they don't feel happy all the time.

Ultimately, it comes down to expectations: The first group saw "well-being" as a state that excluded negative emotions, while the second saw that negative emotions actually had a place in a happy, well-adjusted life. This difference in perception turned out to be a self-fulfilling prophesy! While "happiness" and "positivity" seem pretty similar on the surface, they are quite different approaches. We cannot control the events in our lives or the random moods we fall into or how other people act. We cannot avoid negative feelings around loss or disappointment in life. But we do have control over what we focus on and how we choose to react. *This* is positivity.

So, if you one day feel quite negative or depressed, you might be tempted to think immediately, "This isn't supposed to be this way. I should be happy." You focus on what you feel, and this actually disempowers you further. But you could also think, "This *is* how I feel, and that's just how it is. But I can take steps to make things better right now."

The switch, then, happens when we change focus from how we **feel** or who we are to what we can **do**.

But the *Emotion* study found out more. When we try to increase our "in the moment" happiness, we may also inadvertently make ourselves feel worse for similar reasons—we merely confront again and again a present that doesn't live up to what we think it should be. What's the alternative? According to the authors, take steps today that you willingly know will create happiness for you in the future.

To do this, you can engage in happiness *habits* rather than one-off activities you hope will generate the "right" state of mind right now. When you exercise, reach out to others, act with generosity, or take a few steps toward a future goal, you don't create much immediate happiness in the moment. But what you do is make it far more likely that you'll be happier tomorrow and in the future. This is a question of reframing our happiness project: Rather than focusing on instant gratification, we can rest in the knowledge that we can always take steps in the right direction, laying stones on the pathway to a future that, with each action, looks a little better. So, happiness is more of a by-product of your conscious, repeated, and habitual action than it is a momentary flash of the right chemicals in your brain right in the present moment.

These findings can seem very counterintuitive for those who have been taught to strive constantly for a present moment that is, in essence, perfect. But if we're honest with ourselves, we may see how this perfect moment is more of a harmful fiction than a realistic goal to center in life. Humphrey et al.'s analysis concluded that the key was to value negative emotions rather than to try desperately to avoid them. We can choose to focus on the positive feelings—without denigrating the negative ones.

DOSE Hormones

Let's end our book at the same place we started it: in the brain.

We've explored a range of different activities, approaches, and mindsets that are all associated with happiness—and each and every one of them does so because it induces the release of certain "happy" hormones in the brain. No matter whether it's contentment, joy, bliss, excitement, love, or serenity, all these feelings come from a mix of the four key neurotransmitters (you can remember them by the acronym DOSE):

Dopamine

This enables pleasure, motivation, and learning. It's an important part of the reward mechanism in the brain, but its overstimulation can result in compulsive, addictive behavior.

You can increase dopamine any time you achieve a goal or give yourself a little reward.

Oxytocin

The powerful neurotransmitter responsible for feelings of trust, love, and connection, oxytocin is behind our relationships and sense of social connection. Trust, safety, calmness, and comfort are a big part of happiness, and that is oxytocin's specialty.

Serotonin

The hormone associated with confidence, contentment, and self-acceptance, serotonin bolsters your feelings of significance and can foster feelings of status, loyalty, competence, and power. This is the chemical released when we triumph over challenges, meet our goals, and act with integrity. It's also behind our drive to grow and learn, to improve ourselves, to lead and inspire others, and to feel pride.

Endorphins

These handy chemicals are all about physical euphoria and kick in to mask the temporary effects of pain. Endorphins are your body's way to alleviate stress, anxiety, and physical distress. These natural painkillers are most often associated with the classic "runner's high" but are released during many other forms of exercise.

The way we feel is not purely down to our willpower. Our state of mind, rather, is a result of our neurochemical reality. Without enough dopamine, we can suffer procrastination, low energy and motivation, hopelessness, and low self-esteem. Without oxytocin, we can feel lonely and disconnected and even experience insomnia. Without serotonin, we are at risk for depression, OCD, and social phobia and may find ourselves overly sensitive. Without endorphins, we may experience more aches and pains, mood swings, and impulsive behavior.

With so many of the techniques and treatments we have to treat mental health issues now available, it can be easy to forget that essentially every one of them works because it tweaks the above brain chemicals.

Of course, humans are not machines, and being happy is so much more than simply dialing up this or that neurochemical and waiting for the good feelings to kick in! Instead, we maintain healthy, responsive brains by the lifestyle choices we make and the consistent habits we form. When healthy and supported, our brains will work as they should. We can build happiness from the bottom up:

On a **physical** level by understanding and working with the biology of happiness in our brains and the rest of our bodies.

On a **cognitive** level by working with the thoughts and beliefs we hold.

On an **emotional** level, embracing (all of) our emotions, processing our feelings, and accepting who we are.

On a **practical** level by using consistent habits and our daily lifestyle choices to create the material backdrop for a happy life.

On a **social** level by learning to communicate better and deepen our connections with others.

On a **spiritual** level by exploring meaning and purpose and seeking to position ourselves relative to something bigger than us.

As we've seen, the best interventions are those that address as many levels as possible, since our happiness unfolds all at once, holistically. When we sleep well and exercise, we are better able to regulate our emotions, and this makes us more empathetic and better communicators. When we engage others, we encourage our brains to release oxytocin, which in turn helps us feel more connected and resilient. This allows us to be more giving and generous, which in turn generates powerful feelings of meaning, purpose, and belonging. And this in turn floods our brains with feel-good chemicals!

This means that the quest for happiness has to be a holistic one. Luckily, today we can empower ourselves with techniques that are supported by peer-reviewed scientific evidence. If we understand what makes us happy and why, then we can consciously take control and choose activities that increase our well-being.

A few things to keep in mind:

Happiness is not a single, isolated event but a habit. It's a lifestyle rather than a hack or a trick. Some studies point to meditation, others to nutrition, and still others to things like gratitude journals or giving to charity. Which one is more likely to lead to happiness? Well, *all* of them will! Whatever you choose to include in your daily routine, do it because it makes sense to you, it feels good, and because you understand *why* it works on a neurochemical level. Otherwise, you will merely be running through a checklist of mimicked behaviors, which is not what happiness is about.

To end this book, take a moment to consider for yourself which ideas covered here speak most strongly to you and why. When making changes to your lifestyle, don't think in terms of overnight success and quantum leaps, but rather pick something small you can reliably maintain for the foreseeable future. A small change maintained over years is always worth more than a grand transformation that doesn't last a week. Get your daily dose of DOSE hormones and keep it simple. Finally, go easy on yourself and remember: nobody ever stressed or pressured themselves into being happier!

Summary:

- Many of our assumptions about happiness are wrong. For example, older people have the ability to be happier than younger people, as their emotional regulation ability matures with time, and they focus on quality of life without being overly reactive.
- While playing video games is not usually considered great for mental health, studies show that it is correlated with increased happiness, especially if there's a social element and the games are not addictive.
- Sad movies can make people feel happier, but only if they respond by reflecting on their own relationships in life and correspondingly feel gratitude for what they have.

- Money, too, can buy happiness if it's spent according to our personalities and in the process of creating the life we want and value. We derive more happiness from experiences than from things, and from charity than from spending on ourselves.
- A relentless focus on being happy at all times can backfire and make us miserable and unable to tolerate inevitable negative feelings. Instead, we should focus on being positive and accept our emotions for what they are.
- Prioritizing the future by taking proactive steps in the present is associated with more happiness than "living in the moment."
- Our happiness ultimately comes down to four key neurotransmitters: dopamine, oxytocin, serotonin, and endorphins.
- We can create a happy life for ourselves on multiple levels, using evidence-based research to inform the conscious decisions we make day to day.

Summary Guide

CHAPTER 1: DAILY HABITS FOR HAPPINESS

- Happiness can be tricky to define, but it all starts in the brain. We can turn to scientific peer-reviewed studies to learn the daily habits and mindsets most associated with well-being.
- Though routines are important, so is novelty; make efforts to mix things up now and again and try something new every day.
- Gratitude is strongly associated with feelings of well-being. Say thank you, or simply dwell on all the things you have to be thankful for.
- Try meditation, but remember to approach it without grasping at goals or desired outcomes.
- Try self-affirmation, but focus on affirmations that are value-based rather than those dealing with your traits or performance as a person.
- Get into a reading habit to increase your empathy and communication skills as well as relaxation. Anything goes, but literary

fiction is best for strengthening perspective and "theory of mind" ability.
- Journaling or keeping a diary can make you happier and help you modulate and regulate your emotions. Try whatever form works best for you.
- Finally, understand the role that hope plays in keeping people optimistic and resilient. Always have something to look forward to and you will discover you have endless sources of energy and enthusiasm to draw on. Don't give up!

CHAPTER 2: QUICK HAPPINESS FIXES

- Though happiness is a habit, there are also plenty of immediate happiness "quick fixes" to use when you're feeling low and need something to pick you up.
- One great way to be happy is to use music. Pick songs that are relatively quick in tempo, written in a major key, and have positive and uplifting lyrics.
- You may find that nostalgic music from your past is especially good at summoning up good feelings.

- Studies done on the effect of Botox on people's ability to express and interpret facial expressions point to the interplay between our moods and our biology. Being able to mirror other people's expressions is important. Even though we think we smile because we're happy, we are also happy because we smile. This means we can often create good feelings by smiling—even if we don't quite feel it.
- Ice cream has been shown to be one of the greatest comfort foods that genuinely boosts mood, primarily because of its associations. A healthy diet is best in the long term, but an occasional treat can be a legitimate pick-me-up.
- Recalling happy memories or making new ones has been shown to predict happy feelings.
- Finally, EFT tapping is an approach that can help you alleviate anxiety.

CHAPTER 3: PROVEN HAPPINESS METHODS AND TECHNIQUES

- There are several proven techniques for inducing happiness, one of them being the

inclusion of positive anticipation in life, i.e., making sure you always plan something to look forward to in the future.
- Smartphones can drum up good feelings if you use them to take photos of yourself, something that interests you, or something that will make someone else happy.
- That said, your brain does need a break from screens, and a digital detox or notification-ban can help you relax and unplug, as well as cut down on distractions.
- Screen time is typically associated with negative outcomes, but not all screen time is created equal. Be conscious about the kind of media you consume and why, choosing those things that make you feel better.
- Making or appreciating art is a great way to boost your mood, since it encourages a state of mind not dissimilar to falling in love.
- Declutter mess in your home and you may feel more relaxed and happier. Start small and don't put too much pressure on yourself.
- One way to declutter your digital world is to get rid of unnecessary notifications on your cell phone or other device.

CHAPTER 4: CREATING A HAPPY ENVIRONMENT

- A happy physical environment is a big part of maintaining well-being.
- Get outside and into green spaces, especially natural spaces filled with trees and foliage. Otherwise, try to surround yourself in the peaceful and happy color of nature: green.
- Make sure you're getting enough sleep (eight hours minimum), since the sleep-deprived brain is literally incapable of proper emotional regulation.
- Owning a pet can drastically increase your quality of life, but if that's not practical, find other ways to include furry friends into your day—and that means cat videos, too.
- Try dopamine dressing. There are no rules—simply be mindful about picking items that symbolize joy and happiness for you personally.
- Scents can have a significant effect on our well-being; use scented candles in citrus scents to energize you, or opt for perfumes or cleaning products that you love the smell of or that remind you of happy memories.

- Finally, light your home strategically. Natural light is best, but you can create happy environments with artificial light, too. Studies show that intense light intensifies emotions. Turn down the lights when you need to make important decisions, but turn them up when energy and enthusiasm are flagging.

CHAPTER 5: THE SOCIAL SIDE OF HAPPINESS

- Happiness doesn't occur in isolation but has a real social and relational aspect.
- Even though you may feel that you hate phone calls and prefer texting, connecting via voice is shown to make people far happier.
- Singing makes people happy, but singing together even more so. Join a choir if you can, and you'll feel happier about life—even if you're objectively less well off!
- Cooking and baking have impressive therapeutic benefits, and these can be doubled if you cook with others or share what you make with loved ones.
- The PERMA model explains positive psychologist Dr. Selinger's five-factor

framework for happiness: positive emotions, engagement, relationships, meaning, and achievement. Happiness is lasting when all five factors are drawn on and interconnected.
- Rather than ticking items off a list, happiness is about our unique strengths and values and what the good life looks like for us personally.
- Complaining is associated with unhappiness but not if we are selective and make sure to take action to solve our problems. The complaint sandwich can help others properly hear our concerns.
- Counterfactual thinking can alter our expectations and make us discount the achievements we've made. Instead of dwelling on everything you didn't achieve, try to focus on how things could have been worse!

CHAPTER 6: YOUR BRAIN AND HAPPINESS

- Many of our assumptions about happiness are wrong. For example, older people have the ability to be happier than younger people, as their emotional regulation

ability matures with time, and they focus on quality of life without being overly reactive.
- While playing video games is not usually considered great for mental health, studies show that it is correlated with increased happiness, especially if there's a social element and the games are not addictive.
- Sad movies can make people feel happier, but only if they respond by reflecting on their own relationships in life and correspondingly feel gratitude for what they have.
- Money, too, can buy happiness if it's spent according to our personalities and in the process of creating the life we want and value. We derive more happiness from experiences than from things, and from charity than from spending on ourselves.
- A relentless focus on being happy at all times can backfire and make us miserable and unable to tolerate inevitable negative feelings. Instead, we should focus on being positive and accept our emotions for what they are.
- Prioritizing the future by taking proactive steps in the present is associated with more happiness than "living in the moment."

- Our happiness ultimately comes down to four key neurotransmitters: dopamine, oxytocin, serotonin, and endorphins.
- We can create a happy life for ourselves on multiple levels, using evidence-based research to inform the conscious decisions we make day to day.

Printed in Great Britain
by Amazon